With You Tonight

A Story of My Life

JUDY BOUCHER

With You Tonight

Copyright © 2019 by Judy Boucher. All rights reserved.

No part of this publication may be reproduced, stored in a retrieval system or transmitted in any way by any means, electronic, mechanical, photocopy, recording or otherwise without the prior permission of the author except as provided by USA copyright law.

The opinions expressed by the author are not necessarily those of URLink Print and Media.

1603 Capitol Ave., Suite 310 Cheyenne, Wyoming USA 82001
1-888-980-6523 | admin@urlinkpublishing.com

URLink Print and Media is committed to excellence in the publishing industry.

Book design copyright © 2019 by URLink Print and Media. All rights reserved.

Published in the United States of America
ISBN 978-1-64367-766-8 (Paperback)
ISBN 978-1-64367-765-1 (Digital)

Non-Fiction
09.07.19

CONTENTS

Chapter 1: Dickson 7
Chapter 2: Garden 18
Chapter 3: England 25
Chapter 4: Work 36
Chapter 5: The Band 47
Chapter 6: Daughter 55
Chapter 7: Husband 67
Chapter 8: Post – Marriage 97
Chapter 9: Recording 102
Chapter 10: Crossover 115
Chapter 11: Publicity 124
Chapter 12: National Television 132
Chapter 13: Returning home 143
Chapter 14: Litigation 156
Chapter 15: South Africa 168
Chapter 16: Mom 180
Chapter 17: Politics 187
Chapter 18: Performing 193
Chapter 19: Retirement 201

CHAPTER ONE

Dickson

ST VINCENT, ARE PART OF a chain of islands in the Caribbean. The group stretches from Grenada in the south to St Lucia, the third of four Windward Islands. The fourth is Dominica. While the entire archipelago is referred to as the Grenadines, St Lucia and Dominica, is an independent state. The mainland, St Vincent, is approximately 133 square miles, with a population of just over 110,000. Add in the 'gems of the sister islands', the Grenadines, and the population rises to just over 120,000. I might be biased, but if there are more captivating islands anywhere in the Caribbean, I would gladly pay to visit them.

Mainland St Vincent resembles a heavily pregnant woman. If you imagine her resting on her side, the leeward coast would be her eight-month load, the windward, her spine under serious pressure, as we say in the West Indies. The sea is serene and calm on the leeward side, placid and delightful beneath its rugged volcanic terrain. On the opposite side of the island, however, it rages and pounds the land mercilessly, especially during the hurricane season. Just over half way along the windward side, a mile inland from the main road that clings to the coastline, a tiny village welcomed a beautiful girl into the world.

Time of delivery? Weight? Any special characteristics? I wish I had got at least one of these details from my mother, but, having given birth to so many of us, that might have been expecting too much from her. The first and last might have stayed in her mind, but, unless it had been a difficult birth, those in between must have faded from her memory over time, I imagine.

A neighbour, a slim woman with two glaring nostrils in place of a nose, a condition no one could ever explain, delivered me. She wasn't the village midwife, but she had a reputation as the woman who knew the remedy for every ailment. Colds, flu, headache, cuts and fractures, she possessed the widest and most intimate knowledge of the herbs and bushes in the district. If the official midwife was a mile too far from an impatient baby, mothers were happy to put their faith in this slender woman with no formal training, and who laboured in the fields by day alongside her fellow villagers.

I can still visualize her, this wisp of a woman who 'cabbed' each of us hard on the backside to get us to open our frail lungs. She loved children, I'm sure, but she was also wary of them. In her eyes children were noisy and mischievous, little nuisances to be taught their proper place, even those she had brought into the world. I suppose she had good reason. For as soon as our limbs had developed sufficiently, we would steal into someone's backyard, climb a tree and pluck the fruits that tasted so much sweeter and juicier for being stolen.

To prevent us doing this she would hang a clear bottle with the figure of a man inside it on a branch of her fruit tree to scare us off. Obeah, some of the older children warned, causing our hearts to thump away, the little man would do all sorts of things to us. The hand that picked the fruit might snap off at the shoulder, the guilty fingers might turn blue overnight. The fruit might take root in our stomach, it might sprout branches, they would grow out of our ears and sleeves. Obeah indeed! We were terrified to begin with, but when we realized that it was all nonsense, we got brave and raided the trees on her land as we pleased!

My mother was originally from a tiny corner of our little village. She was a proud woman, the bearer of nine children, five girls and four boys. The fifth of her children, I didn't feel special in any way. The elder children had to take care of the young ones, and I sometimes felt like I was left in the middle without a role.

My father was strong, tall, a man to look up to in every way. He owned some fruit trees next to our neighbour, and we often helped ourselves to the grapefruit, oranges, bananas, plantains and mangoes that covered the acre or so of fertile land. If my early life seems to have been taken up with filling my stomach, then I would plead that I was no different from the scores of children who, in their little groups, raided a tree then sat in the shade of another to share the spoils.

My father lived across the road from my mother's house, an arrangement which didn't strike me then as odd: for which child is concerned with such matters when he or she can spend sunny days playing with friends from dawn till dusk? He worked as a carpenter at the sugar factory, and my earliest memories are of him bringing home half-bottles of salted peanuts and 'bodyline', a tough cake that had to be soaked before you could bite into it. 'Bodyline' was coarse but filling, and, best of all, 'bodyline' was cheap. Cheese and bread were a treat for us children, and my father never disappointed us. I remember that he had a sister, who also lived in the village, but what became of her, I'm afraid I don't know.

Apart from my parents, my eldest sister, was probably the strongest influence on my early life. Ten of us managed to find space in our little 'board house', of the kind that was common to families throughout the village. Our house stood on stilts, a strong gale would have had it dancing like a drunk with five legs.

I imagine that we children 'paired off' somehow, younger with elder and, for good or ill, my eldest sister got me. At age five or so, I can still remember her taking me on a donkey to a fertile tropical garden a little way into the mountains, which produced fruits and vegetables of every kind. Ripe bananas, juicy aromatic mangoes, yellow guavas, passion fruit, tangerines: I ate until my tiny stomach could stretch no further. These visits to the mountains gave me my first taste of watercress, the tiny green buds bobbing and weaving at the edge of a stream. Even now, I still love their crunchiness and slightly peppery taste.

Happy, happy times these were, with my elder sister and her fiancé! Her 'young man' and future husband, always accompanied us, and it is testimony to their love that they are still together to this day.

Being older, and responsible for looking after us, she made sure that we carried home baskets of dasheen, yams, tannias, plantains, maugh-faugh-baugh and other food that were our staple diet. She knew, also, that we could sell these produce for the corned beef and bread that we loved.

Looking back I can see that mine was a typical childhood in where I am from in the 1950s or indeed the Caribbean, from the accounts of my friends from the other islands. In no way did I think of my family as poor or disadvantaged. We didn't have a lot of money, I knew even then, but we ate well and were happy. Our small board house stood proudly on family land, ten of us crammed into three rooms without a single word of complaint. And it was a similar picture with the neighbours to our left and right, and for those in front and behind. Green bananas, yam and breadfruit were plentiful; neighbours shared when their land bore a good crop, the fowls that roamed in the yard provided our supply of meat. No one in our close community could complain of going hungry, for sugar cane, mangoes other fruits were abundant, only the lazy or drunk wore sour faces.

The adults in the village looked after us children, scolding us if we got out of line. That was the way then, and still is today, but to a lesser extent. They informed our parents if they caught us doing something especially naughty, they chased us if they thought we were getting up to mischief that could land us in serious trouble. No child would dream of passing an adult without saying 'Good Morning' or

'Good Afternoon', for fear of the look or the beating they would get when their parents found out about this lack of 'manners'.

But the adults were more than people who told on children who didn't have 'manners' or 'behaviour'. They cared for us, I could see now, although I didn't then, they wanted a better life for us than they had been given. Most of them worked long hours in the fields weeding, planting and digging yams and arrowroot, or cultivating bananas for a miserable wage. Determined to pass on the knowledge that had seen them through tough times, they enforced discipline and insisted on good 'manners' and respect. A child without those qualities was one to avoid; in their eyes, such a child had already started on a slippery downward slope. We were to learn to enjoy ourselves; they were clear in their minds although they didn't think to tell us, we were to appreciate life, to 'study our books', to learn to be content. But most of all, we were to be happy.

On moonlit nights throughout SVG at the time, the sense of magic and wonder touched the dullest child. The moon cast its light so low and bright that it might have been the middle of the afternoon. Like childbirth, such a night is one of the wonders of this beautiful world. These precious nights, before widespread television and radio, still linger lovingly in my memory. What joyful singing, what a beautiful noise we made! Even now their power can bring tears to my eyes. Children and adults sang old folk songs together, they played 'ring play', we got to see our parents throw off the cares of work, of failing or fading relationships, of the struggle to make ends meet.

Old rhymes, nonsense stories, suggestive and lewd songs, what a pity so many have been lost. 'The man in the moon, oh, was digging potato', 'Miss Caine had a baby', 'Jane and Louisa', songs handed down over generations. Villagers chanted at the top of their voices merrily before falling asleep, two or three to a bed, with one under the bed if the family was especially large. Dickson village was like that. We were deliriously happy in our world, mingling easily on moonlit nights, gazing in wonder at the trillions of stars that blazed in the night sky, sure that somewhere in the vastness, there were people just like us, marvelling at the heavens.

We children played 'pound stone', where you had to be extremely quick or your neighbour's stone would crash down on the back of your hand. At dusk we played 'coop', where we would hide in some shady spot in the village praying that we wouldn't be found. 'Corkins' was a favourite game. We would make a 'ball' from whatever material was available and pelt it at one of the players with all the force which our young hands could muster. The lime or grapefruit wrapped in a bit of cloth would sting the victim's back, and we would scream with laughter until we got hit ourselves. Some children cried from the blow but most enjoyed this bit of harmless fun.

Each child in the village had a nickname, as did the adults. If someone caught you eating a fig they might call you 'Fig' and the name might stick. A child who wet the bed might be known as 'Piss-a-bed', one who was greedy would go by the name of 'Pang gut'. I can't remember what my nickname was, although I must have had one.

Both my parents worked hard, all the adults did. In the fields digging arrowroot, planting yams and weeding, tending to bananas to ship to England or cutting plantains and other produce for the market. I suppose my parents were luckier than most. They were spared the fields and toiling under the sting of the midday sun that prematurely wrinkled the face and hands of the other villagers. The intensity of the sun seemed to suck the blood from some of the workers, it sapped their strength, each year of toil added to the dragging of their hardened and calloused soles. My father made the short journey to the sugar factory each day, but my mother had a longer walk to earn a living.

There was a magnificent estate property in town from a wealthy family with lavish lifestyle. They were the type that could afford to import an E-type Jaguar, so we are talking about serious money here.

My mother worked in the great house and my earliest memories are of her rolling home so tired late at night that she would fall asleep with her dinner on her lap. When she recovered, she would feed us the stories of the meals the guests took and the amount they drank, and we would listen and pray that one day we too could own a grand house with servants and maids. The leftovers from the feasts ended up in our grateful stomachs, and we wished they would have a banquet every day, not realising that this would take its toll on our dear mother.

Like many other West Indians before, and the thousands who would follow, my elder sister left for a 'better life' in England when I was young. Her leaving didn't really register with me, for I was too young to understand its significance. One night she invited her friends and neighbours to share a meal, the next day there was a gaping hole in our lives.

The eldest sister, who was seventeen, had to help to look after us now, and she took to the task without complaint or grumble. My younger sister, helped too, looking after everybody. They prepared our meals, washed our clothes, and got us ready for school. But a few months after my seventh birthday, my mother, too, had a gathering at the house with food and drink aplenty, and before I could grasp what was happening, she too was off to England.

With the two people I was closest to gone, it was now up to my two elder siblings, and to some extent, my brother had to look after us. I got on with my little chores – washing the dishes, fetching firewood, sweeping the yard – but something was definitely missing in my life. I was too young to put a name to it, but it was obvious to me that my situation had changed; and even more terrifying, that I had no choice but to get used to it.

The task I looked forward to more than any other around this time was going to the post office in Georgetown to collect the stiff blue and white striped envelope my mother mailed monthly from England with our allowance. Even now I can still feel the firmness of the envelope in my little hands, the stiff edges sharp against the fingers. You couldn't beat the feverish excitement of a registered letter. We queued at the post office for days in the hope of hearing our name called out by the postmaster. If we were disappointed twice, the third day was bound to be our lucky one. And I was, month after month. For I knew that tucked inside the blue letter saying how much she missed us would be a twenty-pound postal order which would soon turn into crisp purple twenty-dollar notes. That pristine smell of rustling notes: can you ever beat it?

At school I didn't stand out. I made no impression on the teachers, and it would be stretching the truth to say I have fond memories of a single one. Even the names have gone. No female member saw anything but another village girl; to the male staff I was probably invisible. Many of those who drew their monthly wages were happy to let children drift unless they were exceptionally bright. I wasn't a dunce, was not rude like some of the boys, or aggressive, so they probably didn't regard me as someone to work with. Where others of my generation have fond memories of their teachers and those who had an influence on their early lives, I don't remember being praised for a good piece of arithmetic or scolded by one because I hadn't done myself justice in a story I had hastily scribbled.

Apart from teaching me to read and count, school didn't have any significant impact on the young me. It was a place where children were sent, or had to go to, so I obeyed the ritual. No one took the time to point out that a good education could open up possibilities; the teachers at our school didn't search for the talent within a child and try to nurture it. They were a sour lot, as far as my memory would allow me to recall them. A child with a talent for singing or reciting poetry would have escaped their notice, who knows what might have happened if I had gone to a primary school where teachers saw themselves as people with a mission to draw out the goodness in their charges and truly inspire them.

Being an obedient child, I must have recited the times tables and had my nails and hair inspected before entering the school building; but the lessons must have washed over me. What I do recall clearly is being taunted by other children. They mocked my 'red complexion', calling me 'red head', 'picky head' or 'dry head', 'mulatto'. Their teasing nearly drove me to cry several times, but I held out; I wasn't going to give them that satisfaction.

Yet it hurt. The taunts, the mocking, the funny looks; how I wished that my mother or elder sister were around to protect me from their cruel mockery. A word from either of them would have put the naughty children in their place. But, despite their dreadful behaviour I knew that life had to go on. I scrambled home at midday for my lunch of lime juice and bread, I ran back for afternoon lessons under the full glare of the sun. Dad continued to bring us food, I especially liked the cheese and salami, our lives in the village trickled by as if it would never change.

What about my singing? At the time I had no idea that this would play such an important part in my future. My brother was the one with the voice and my mother was quite good too, humming her hymns and serenading us when the mood took her. We are a musical family though; it is simple now to trace the source of this gift. My younger brother has his own band in Fifth Street. My brothers would put together a band in England, but I would have laughed at anyone who suggested that one day she would earn a living from music. To suggest that her name would be recognized by Europeans, South Africans and Brazilians might have terrified her.

Like the other children, I loved to listen to the rousing services at the gospel hall in the village. Only the deaf or stone-hearted could fail to be moved by the power of their songs. And which child isn't struck by the way a tune could draw in a 'converted' congregation and drive them into a trance? The little plays they put on at school made a strong impression on me too, but watch, listen and applaud, that was me. Taking part in performing or singing was not even a dream: I was happier as a member of the audience, centre stage was for those whose talents screamed out.

So my life as a young girl from a small village rolled slowly on. Hot days, stifling evenings, nights when you had to leave the windows open for fear of suffocating. Rainy days as well, the raindrops like dull nails thudding against the roof. Storms and high winds during the hurricane season, being stuck indoors, feeling restless, praying for the dry times to come round again, my days and nights obeyed the seasons, and I fell in like the obedient child I was.

I had my friends no matter what the weather, and my siblings were close by should anything happen. At weekends or during the school holidays I went to the mountains with my brother to dig yams or to gather aromatic nutmegs whose smell I can still conjure up 60 years later. We would fish for mullets, lobsters and crayfish in 'Texeira Deep Hole' one day, and my brother would lay traps for manicou the next. Back then there was no hunting season so it was open season all year round. I preferred the days when he placed the traps, for which child doesn't enjoy watching and listening to a humming iron pot of flour, bananas and manicou?

Manicou are a protected species now, but back then when there were more trees, I suppose, they were plentiful. I'm not sure that I would eat one now but as a child, manicou was a delicious treat. To trap one of the little delicacies Ben would cut a bunch of banana, dig a deep hole in the field and gently lower the bunch to the bottom to ripen there. Attracted by the smell, my brother explained, a manicou would crawl down the hole to feed on the bananas. For some reason I didn't understand, they couldn't climb back up from the hole. The steepness of the sides or their short front feet, I don't know which. The explanation didn't make sense to me. What I do remember is the feeling of anticipation when Ben had trapped one and the thought of a bubbling pot on three firestones in the yard later that evening. The crunchiness of the manicou, the soup with a little butter and a hint of black pepper: what more could a young girl ask for?

Unfortunately, however, like my mother and elder sister, my brothers too would disappear to England and my girlhood would grow more bewildering.

But in time the memories of Mom and elder sister faded. When you are in the Caribbean surrounded by your friends, when you look out at the distant horizon and the blue sea fades into a silvery-white, cold Europe seems to belong to a different universe. Loved ones gradually lose their pull; you are like estranged lovers living separate but full lives.

And I was loving my life, simple and lacking in incident as it was. As a child I could roam the village as I pleased, my stomach was never empty for long, what was the point in worrying about a country seemingly a million miles away? There were always other children to play with and even when it rained, our days were never dull. I don't remember a single homicide or violent killing in our village or in the wider district, or a funeral. Not in all my years there. It was as though this narrow life would continue forever. The sun beat down upon us, when it got too hot we drifted down to the river to cool off, or to dip our toes in the sea. My mother and my sister belonged to a different world now, and I was to follow them. But only after a detour that still makes me shiver to this day.

CHAPTER TWO

Garden

WHEN I WAS TEN I went to live with an aunt. Then as now, it wasn't unusual for children to take off with a relative for a different village. A boy in danger of falling in with the wrong crowd might be dispatched to another district for his own good, a girl growing up too fast, for her protection. There was always an old uncle requiring a companion to help farm his land or look after his shop, or a widow in search of a young girl to alert the neighbours in case she fell ill during the night; the benefits were obvious to all. A family rarely turned down a request. But my aunt wasn't old, so did I need protection? No one set out the reasons before me. All I remember is finding myself in this new home with an aunt I had been introduced to on the day of my departure.

Her husband was an architect. He must have earned a lot if he could afford a big place in such prime surroundings. I didn't see much of him, but my aunt was ever present. From the beginning I felt uncomfortable with the arrangement. I struggled to fit in; town life just wasn't for me. The freedom of my tiny village had been cruelly snatched; I was to endure some of the unhappiest days of my childhood.

I had been free in Dickson as children are in villages everywhere. From the moment I got up the day was mine to spend as I pleased. In the holidays if my friends wanted to play 'coop' or hopscotch, then we did, hour after hour until we got tired, hungry or bored with our freedom. We roamed the village in search of ripe mangoes or plumrose to steal, we chased chickens, we shooed droopy-eyed old dogs into the scorching midday sun, if some grumpy old man or woman chased us from their yard it was no bother, we simply tried our luck elsewhere. Mischief was what children were made for, we told ourselves, it was part of growing up. When you fell out of a tree, bruised your knees or tripped over, you dusted yourself off ready for the next tumble. Unless you were ill or the rain was beating down, you made for outdoors. There was none of this where my aunt lived, neither freedom nor adventure for children.

My aunt had six children, all younger than me. The house was large and well-furnished but, even though I had my own room I felt like a stranger, an outsider. I believed then that I had been sent to her home as a relative but, in reality, I was a 'house girl'. The tasks my older sisters had done for me became my duties now. I had relied on my siblings almost totally but I was forced to grow up fast, taking on responsibilities for which I wasn't prepared. A pupil at a nearby school at the time, I didn't get much time for reading, study or homework…no wonder I didn't become a scholar! The moment I got home I had to get changed and get going. I had to make myself useful. There was the washing to do and ironing, to this day I hate ironing more than any domestic task in the world.

I didn't feel part of the family. In all the time there I considered myself an intruder, not a girl in the company of relatives. My aunt's children eyed me suspiciously and I was too timid to ask them why. There was little banter between us, none of the teasing and play that sealed a relationship. Mock fights, the tugging of clothes, the rolling of the eyes, the hiding of a favourite shirt or skirt, in Dickson these had been some of our favourite children pastimes. They tightened our friendships, bonded us, although we didn't think of these activities in this way. Nothing like this happened where I lived before; it was as if play had been outlawed or seen as something to be frowned on.

What my aunt's children thought of me I didn't know. Perhaps they saw me as the intruder I felt like. I took my meals at a separate table; I ate in silence while the family enjoyed each other's company. A police relative came to visit one afternoon, I remember, and he was invited to eat at the dining table while I sat in the corner with my plate on my tiny table. That hurt, it really did. I was the one supposed to be living there, but a guest was more important than me! I prayed each night for an end to this segment of my life.

I was studying at a school that time, the qualification you gained after eight,

nine or even 10 years at school. For those who had to re-sit the examination –and there were many, boys as well as girls – you could attempt it even when you were 16. Maths and English were the main subjects, Hygiene also, and possibly Religious Education, I'm not sure. History might have been part of it too but British History, I would imagine, little of the Caribbean in those unenlightened days. The biology they taught was basic, avoiding the very things teenage boys and girls most needed to know: as I was to discover in my third year.

One night when I was 13, I was in bed when this sudden pain gripped me. It was like nothing I had experienced before. The pain was excruciating, my stomach felt as if it was being sliced from the inside by a dull knife. Something seemed to be seizing my internal organs, knotting them, tearing them apart. I might have screamed, I might have cried, I can't remember. I thought I was going to die that night, I wanted to die.

If you gashed your sole on a broken bottle you screamed for blue murder, but a trip to the hospital and a good night's sleep took care of the pain. The feelings I had that night were a thousand times more excruciating than a cut, a stumped toe, or a tumble from the branch of a fruit tree. The cause of the pain from a cut or fall was obvious, the remedy too. But this affliction had arrived without warning, what I had done wrong, I wondered?

After a fitful night, when I woke up the next morning, I rolled over and my eyes went directly to the bloody sheets. A red island had formed and my lower half was in a state. A new panic gripped me. What should I do, where could I hide my panties and the sheet? But there was nowhere to hide them. Had it been our house in Dickson I would have found a way and a place, but not in a stranger's house?

I didn't say anything to my aunt, I was afraid of what she might say or accuse me of. In my ignorance I could picture her grumbling that I had deliberately soiled the bed, I tried to think of how I was going to explain something I didn't understand myself. But when she discovered the bedclothes, she wasn't angry as I had feared, just a little taken aback by their state: they had been crumpled and torn from the wriggling and twisting and the friction of my feet when the pain struck. In her mind she must have envisaged the agony I had gone through. 'You're a young woman now DD,' she said to me without explaining fully what she meant, 'you mustn't play with boys.'

'You mustn't play with boys'. Nowadays a mother or aunt would sit a girl down and reassure her that what she was experiencing was natural, nothing to be ashamed of or to feel guilty about. But 50 years ago? It was almost taboo. I suppose most girls were well and truly on their own. You learned through whispers, you learned from rumour. If you were unfortunate you learned too late, from painful experience. That night still haunts me, and I would not wish the experience on another young girl. I can remember the expression on Mrs Smith's face, and her warning as though it was yesterday.

My other sister visited not long after this, I remember. 'you developing,' she observed, with a coarse chuckle. I didn't care for her observation, especially the way she said it. Where my aunt had had a warning all she could do was mock the changes in my young body. And this from a sibling! Being terribly self-conscious, I tried to hold myself in, to pretend that I was the same girl who had left Dickson for town a few years earlier. But, like it or not, I had grown, and the monthly pains were a part of my 'development'. Some girls have it easy, I was one of those who had it bad.

When my aunt noticed me doubling up in agony one month, she prepared a potion whose foul taste still makes me squirm to this day. Where she got it from, she never said. It might have been from her mother but she didn't share such things with me: we were never that close. A black worm with 'thorns', a 'cheff' worm that lived on a certain unknown plant, was the basis of the dreadful mixture. She would lower the worm into a small bottle of rum or brandy to cure for my time of the month! I squeezed my eyes tight while I swallowed, I pinched my nose to avoid the disgusting smell. I was to leave her house not knowing if she drank the same foul medicine or if she gave it to her daughters. I also left without knowing the result of my school examination.

For, one day, some two years later, my aunt announced that my mother had sent for me. My siblings emigrated after my move to join her; it was my turn to join the rest of my family in England. I was happy, but not delirious. The breathless excitement other children felt on hearing such wonderful news remained buried inside me. It was as if I had lost the capacity for joy. The years away from my village seemed to have driven out the sense of fun in the teenage DD. If you don't have your friends around to share good news, it feels like winning a consolation prize instead of the first prize.

As in my previous school, the pupils at my school mocked the complexion my father passed down to me. 'Aberdee', mulatto, 'dry head', they teased me and ran away. Instead of giving as good as I got I usually stood there feeling stupid and awkward. I was hypersensitive, I suppose, and it didn't occur to me that sometimes insults are another child's invitation to begin a friendship. When the taunts for dye. My red hair had to go, I decided, I wanted it black and ordinary so that I would fit in with my schoolmates. Naturally my mother refused this stupid request. Did my foolish letter influence my mother's decision? I don't know but, several months later, when Mrs Smith gave me the news that my mother had sent for me, the thought briefly crossed my mind. got too much I wrote to my mother asking My aunt must have got me ready, arranging for me to get my passport and other travel documents. She had looked after me, it was only fair to give me the send-off I deserved. Nowadays a trip by plane is commonplace, but in the 60s it represented glamour, the highest kind of adventure. There would have been my hair to do and a new dress to ensure that I made a good impression on landing. Gloves too, I imagine, and a hat and a pretty little handbag.

For no one would have dreamt of entering the mother country dressed in the causal way we see today. No jeans, T-shirt or trainers; it was something new, nothing borrowed, it was the level above your Sunday best for the people greeting you at the airport. A photograph taken when I was 15 shows me with my hair straightened, a slight girl looking slightly bemused: that's how I must have felt on the trip to the airport -relieved, slightly anxious, and yet quietly excited and with a hint of a smile. Did my aunt hug me? Was she sorry to see me go? I don't know, I can't remember; and the opportunity to ask has been lost with her passing. I might have shed a quiet tear, she might have dabbed the corner of her eyes, but all that has been lost, I'm afraid.

What would have become of me had my mother not sent for me, I sometimes wonder? If I had stayed and passed my school certificate, where would I be today? Older children who passed this demanding exam trained to be primary school teachers, those who could afford the transfer fees to a secondary school for higher study. Would my aunt have supported me? Would I have enjoyed life as a teacher in charge of dozens of mischievous children? Would I have tried to nurture pupils to make up for what my primary school teachers failed to do?

And my musical career, how might that have gone had I not come to England? Would the chain of events that led to me recording have had some parallel? Would someone have popped up, seen the flame that needed fanning, and taken the trouble to coax it into a blaze? There were steel bands that played at carnival in SVG at the time, but recording was still in its infancy. From what I can gather from those who were familiar with the music scene then, female singers were few, singing was a male preserve. Calypsonians spent the year composing their songs, but events were local, not centered on the capital as they are now. No singer or musician at the time made a living from his craft. Even today with the wealth of marketing at their disposal, only a handful of musicians or singers are full time.

When I was a girl, a famous singer at that time serenaded villagers with his witty tunes, but even he couldn't survive on the proceeds. What might have happened had I stayed I can only speculate about.

CHAPTER THREE

England

I LEFT DICKSON FOR KINGSTOWN when I was ten and never returned to the village. Years would pass before I would go back. I lost contact with my little friends and saddest of all, I never saw my father again. He had done what he could for me but he had set up home in Chili, a village about three miles and a half from Dickson, with a woman, I was told. They were a family of two, happy and I wished them well when I heard the news. But I missed him then and I wish now that I had gotten to know him better. For which girl doesn't miss her dear father? Who doesn't lament missing out on one half of her heritage? But I was miles away struggling to come to terms with my new life, living each long day not knowing what was going to happen next. I suppose I secretly held on to the hope that he might suddenly appear one day to rescue me when I lived with my aunt.

Quiet and shy, I was a girl from a tiny village; I needed conversation and play to bring me out of myself. But where my aunt lived wasn't designed for children. It wasn't a village, and I didn't have many playmates. No Anansi stories, no tales of ghosts and 'rounces' to keep me up at night wondering if a spirit might fly through the window in the middle of the night. While my old classmates back in Dickson were probably out under the moonlight gazing at the stars, I sat gloomily indoors with just myself for company. And who wants to be with herself when she is young, full of energy and craving mischief?

My aunts' children went to the 'prep' school, the private school in Frenches where the professionals, politicians and well-to-do of the island sent their precious offspring. The school is still there, a flat, modest structure, a seat of privilege easily dismissed as just another structure as you walk past. My aunt's children probably looked down on me but what did I care now that my flight had been paid for? I was going to England, I could 'break style' on them for the first time: they could keep their fancy school uniform and cap. If they asked me to write to them, I would fabricate the most wonderful tales and adventures.

How did I feel about my mother's request to join her? I felt excited, yes, and I can remember feeling relived that I was to see her again after such a long time. I was beginning to feel adrift, alone, with no true friends to share little secrets. On the faces of the girls in my class I saw the brightness and joy of children secure within their families; such happy black faces, why was mine glum so much of the time? My mother's request came at just the right time. It probably saved me from the haphazard lives less unfortunate girls got sucked into, quickly spiralling out of control, degenerating into drink and, in some cases, even worse.

Where my aunt lived have some of the most spectacular views on the island. To the west there is the enchanting view of the harbour of the capital, Kingstown, charming, magical, like a painting that can shock you with its pure beauty. Due south, the tiny island of Bequia springs magically from the sea and challenges you to swim the nine miles when the weather is calm. Rising majestically to the north I can still picture the beautiful hill where our national hero Chatoyer fought his final battle with the English. Being young and ignorant I took these natural features for granted: when you wake up and the blue water of the harbour shimmers enticingly; when the lush greenery pleasures your eyes throughout the year, it is only natural to grow complacent. It is only when I was thousands of miles away that I missed the splendour of the landscape and the familiar things that brightened my days there.

And I was to miss them sorely during the first year in England. The sights and smells of the village, the sea, the sweet-smelling hibiscus, the aroma of the fruit trees, the colourful butterflies that seemed to follow me to school and escort me home. The deadly Jack Spaniards, too, even though they built their nests in the galvanized zinc ceiling of our home in Dickson, waiting for a victim to lance (sting) by the eyes or the exposed wrist. Every country was like this, I had assumed, with insects fluttering harmlessly in search of victims to sting, and dogs chasing you until the heat got the better of them when they limped, tongues licking the left side of their mouths, to the shade of the nearest tree.

I had assumed that I was going to live in a house surrounded by trees laden with fruit whose aroma rushed into the house the moment the front door or a window was opened. Huge, magical houses, then, each on its own plot flanked by mango and orange trees, and with a couple of cars parked at the front waiting to rush me to London. I pictured myself in a swimsuit at the beach in some English town, diving into the warm sea, then skipping along the hot black sand shouting at the top of my voice for the sheer fun of it. Small streams trickling lazily along, the hot sun blazing each day, I would have argued with anyone who suggested that there were countries where the sea was hundreds of miles from your town, or where the rivers were wide enough to take large ships. England was to give me the shock of my life.

I'm ashamed to say that I don't remember much of the journey itself to England, the short 'hop' to Barbados from what was then the only airport, then the long night flight northeast across the Atlantic from Barbados. With a little encouragement, some of my female friends can conjure up images of straightening their hair, of powdering themselves, one or two can even remember the price of their new shoes. For the men, in the days leading up to their departure, it was a case of seeking out the slickest barber after they had been to Kingstown to select the most expensive trousers, shirts and shoes they could afford. My memories are vague and sometimes I curse myself for that. The preparations, the final goodbye to my home, the aircraft taxiing gingerly along the runway, one of these days I must try to reach these deep recesses of memory to discover what else they might contain.

Male or female, even at that age, my friends appreciated that they were leaving home for good. I did too I'm sure, but without their full-blown conviction. The journey was to be one-way; no one could name a single person who had made the trip to England and returned to SVG. It was goodbye to all we had known. Like clocks adjusted in the Spring to British Summer Time, we set our minds forward, knowing that we would be at the mercy of events.

The first requirement for the trip to England was a solid 'grip', a suitcase capable of withstanding an explosion. Some people have stored their old trusty suitcase in the loft, I'm one of those who have discarded this precious item of history. Packed with my earthly belongings, I suppose that it stood proudly by the door for my few well-wishers to see, if indeed there were any. And on the day, it would have been loaded into the taxi, for everyone knew the importance of making a grand exit, one that those present would never forget.

The picture of our departure lodged in the memory of well-wishers was to be one of inspiring awe; my friends assured me that they were careful to set the scene. A warm evening with food and drink for guests, the smells and fuss and self-importance magnified 10 times over. Powder, coconut oil for the limbs and body, perhaps even a hint of lipstick: 'She really look nice, her dress prettier than anything they have in England'. 'England never see a cotton shirt like his, everybody will want one'. We were setting out on a great adventure, it was clear to us - a flight on the fabled BOAC airplane seen on the newsreels at the cinema, new places, people of many nationalities. My preparations were simple, so low-key that little has stuck in the memory. There might have been visitors, perhaps several pupils from the local school…but the night itself is still something of a blur.

My situation wasn't unique, I mustn't give that impression. Dozens of girls would have been in exactly the same position, some setting out from the family home, others from that of a relative or friend. England was rebuilding after the Second World War and it had decided to recruit people from the Caribbean. The majority were from Jamaica but, eventually the smaller islands added to the quota. Many of our people had fought in the war, but the link was far stronger: at least 300 years of one-sided history, according to the books we studied in the senior forms at school back home where my aunt lives. We were going home, then, some went as far as saying, believing foolishly that the Caribbean links with the mother country were the strongest of all her former colonies.

So, up to the seventies, one parent left for England, normally the father. In due course he sent for his wife, and the children followed when the family had saved enough, or had found suitable accommodation. In my case, my mother played the role my father would have played had they been together. Hundreds of young girls had made the journey before and now, after a harrowing five years, it was my turn. I was the traveler, the one with her sights set on new horizons! The sense of adventure might have been set on Low, but deep in my tiny bosom, I don't doubt the quiet feeling of happiness there must have been.

An Englishman was in charge of me for the eight-hour leg of the flight from Barbados to England. A chaperone, I suppose I should call him, do they still have them nowadays? The aircraft would have departed late in the evening, say, seven o'clock, and, taking into account the five hours' time difference, it would have arrived in London around six, if not earlier. The man must have taken his job seriously for I don't recall a single hitch. He must have encouraged me to sample the strange-looking food, although what I had to eat remains a mystery to me. I can imagine him making sure the blankets covered me snugly to keep out the cold of altitude, I can picture him reassuring me when there was a spot of turbulence. This anonymous man would have patiently guided me through immigration and escorted me into the grateful arms of my mother in Arrivals. I hope I thanked him for his kindness and patience. If I was too overwhelmed by the whole experience, I'm sure my mother would have made up for the oversight.

We landed in late summer but it felt cold at Heathrow. I was freezing. For someone accustomed to temperatures constantly above eighty, sixty and even seventy are positively arctic. Peering out of the small oval window of the aircraft I saw what I thought was smoke. I gasped, I remember that. Smoke, fire, was there something wrong, I wondered? Had I travelled three thousand miles just to end up in a furnace? It was a light fog, I was told, even in summer it wasn't unusual to find a slight blanket of fog in the early morning. Mist, fog, smog, I would have to get used to these strange facets of the British weather. But on that first morning it felt as if the plane had deposited me on another planet. Surely mist belonged to Caribbean mountaintops, I told myself, not at ground level!

Later, on the journey home, this sense of being dumped onto an alien planet grew even more acute. The England I was experiencing was nothing like the Caribbean. Colours, temperature, the sheer size of the place were alarming. To my young eyes fields stretched to the horizon, the roads were packed with vehicles. And then there were the buildings. The houses resembled factories, huddled together, seizing every available plot. Through the car windows I stared open-mouthed at the crisscrossing roads as though they were 'gashes', wounds, in the lush green fields. And, as for the trees, if they were so bare, why hadn't they been cut down, I wondered?

My mother came to the airport to meet me. She didn't drive but, in the excitement and confusion I can't remember who had done her the favour. We hadn't seen each other since 1958 when I was a mere seven. She was emotional, I recall, and at first I could only stare at the woman who had brought me into the world then disappeared before I could begin to ask the difficult questions every child inevitably has. But it was such a wonderful feeling to be hugged: to feel the warmth of an embrace, to know that someone truly cared for me.

I wanted to bare my soul, to tell her what I had been through, to relate how lonely and unsettling the last five years where my aunt lived. And, in return, I wanted to know everything about England, there and then, all at once. But, after the initial greetings, Mom and I were like strangers. We couldn't help the awkward silence that followed. We had hugged, yes, and she had kissed me, but eight years was over half my life! Inevitably the memories of her I carried had grown hazy, and, with so many children to care for, I'm sure she must have felt the same. We would have to learn about one another again, slowly, like a patient recovering after a major operation.

Looking back now, the England of my first year presented a foggy, smoky canvas; grim in many ways. Pollution was rife, it was as though a cigarette factory had been set alight, and all its workers given a license to smoke to their heart's content. Dense and choking, everywhere I went a blanket of smoke and fog hovered menacingly. You couldn't breathe, you couldn't see where you were going at times. It might have been Victorian England. Factories belched their filth, houses poured their smoke to add to this stifling cloud, it was horrible, we are so fortunate now.

The houses were strange, unlike anything we have in the West Indies. To my eyes they were grey, dull, this one resembled its neighbour and the buildings lacked character. Our simple house had stood on our land supported by sturdy wooden pillars, no great beauty but it managed to retain some individuality. Here and there the richer village families built 'wall houses' of yellow, pink or lime green, but to have a house resembling another would have invited ridicule. In England the houses seemed to have been constructed to support one another, packed so tightly that I imagined that if one of them wobbled in a high wind the others might collapse like a pack of dominoes. When I saw smoke swirling from virtually every home, I knew for certain that I was indeed in another world.

In my childish imagination I had expected rivers, the sea, and searing heat. Winter was unknown to me, the idea of seasons took me quite a while to get my head round, I'm not ashamed to admit. In my naivety I had thought of England as perhaps twice the size of SVG with the sun blazing in the sky, strutting in the morning before giving way suddenly with the arrival of dusk. That was all I knew, bright sunshine, then dusk hurling a mighty cloak over the land. I had expected heavy rains during the long school holidays with sun and heat the rest of the year. But the reality soon dawned on me. England dwarfed the tiny islands of SVG, buildings and roads were on an altogether different scale, the climate would set you a new test each year. But, worst of all, the sun England came with was weak, a frail, pitiful cousin of our Caribbean blazer!

My family lived in Fifth Street, where I was to spend most of my life. The town had gained the reputation as the home of Vincentians abroad. Some claim that it has the highest number of Vincentians outside SVG, beating off the challenges of Brooklyn in the United States and Toronto, Canada. Why this so no one seems to know. The original immigrants were attracted by the furniture trade some of the early settlers say, others suggest that it was 'chosen' because it reminded the first visitors of the hilly terrain of the islands. The truth is probably simpler. In the early days people needed contacts, a home and bed in a foreign land; who would they trust but someone they had known from 'home' or someone recommended to them by a friend or relative?

Today's visitors to the shopping center which is the main shopping complex in Fifth Street, descend on a modern space designed for an increasingly affluent population. People travel from far and wide for the attractions and luxuries of the top department stores.

Fifth Street isn't going to be left behind neighbouring Uxbridge, Oxford, Luton or Reading. The cinema delivers escape and the latest blockbusters and there are restaurants and bars for every taste. How different things were in the 60s! A cinema in Frogmoor, Tesco to its left, where I first saw an escalator, Woolworths, Murrays and Marks and Spencer: these were all we had. Quiet and sleepy, the high street was crowned with pubs every hundred yards. If you fancied a livelier experience you had to head for the A40 to London!

Roger's Road, a short walk from the town centre, was where many West Indian families started out in Fifth Street, and it was my first home too. There is nothing special about it but at the time I thought it was Coronation Street, the long-running television programme. Some of the properties were private, but many had been rented out to families like ours. Many other nationalities lived there, Italians, Polish and Asian. The one hundred and thirty-four-bedroom houses gave a view of the big factory and the gentle hills of Downley. The factory has since been demolished to make way for university accommodation, but for years it provided employment for scores of West Indians, if not exotic scenery. When I drive past now, I see that houses have sprung up where once the hills of Downley were lined with trees... times change, we have no choice but to go along with it.

Where my mom lived, we had our neighbours and their families. Soon I would be reunited with my siblings and with my brother-in-law and my niece and nephews. There were people I knew from home and some I would meet for the first time. I was to discover two new siblings, also English-born. My relatives were delighted to see me, and knowing that they were close by was a great comfort as I tried to settle in. When the family got together, I thought of my siblings that were still in Dickson and would soon make the journey I had successfully completed, and my elder sister who, for reasons I could never fathom, didn't wish to come to England.

That summer day, then, Mom pulled up at this nondescript semidetached after what seemed an eternity and, wedged into an oversized coat that would take an age to feel comfortable in, I was shown to my room. Strange, perplexing, but so far so good until I realized that it wasn't my room but our room. I was dumbfounded. We were to share a space that could barely hold two adults!

Was this really England, I asked myself? Was this the place where everyone was supposed to own a car? Was this the country where the crammed fridges were reputed to be as tall as a fully-grown heifer? After the initial shock, though, this arrangement didn't bother me. We had slept two to a bed before, I would soon get used to it. Besides, who but an ungrateful child would argue about a lack of space when they are with the people they care for most of all in the world? And, wasn't the warmth of two greater than that of one?

But life in England took some getting used to, I must admit. Simple things I had never had to think about now mattered. I had to get used to wearing several layers of clothes, their weight bore down on my tiny shoulders forcing me to stoop like an old woman carrying the burden of her years. Food was frozen, it took a day to prepare and eat a chicken. You were locked indoors for a large part of the day; people whispered instead of shouted and heat was artificial in the place I would call home for so many years.

Cars were wedged on both sides of the street and there was a constant hum of traffic. It took me a fortnight to discover the neighbours' name and nationality; everyone seemed to be in a hurry or had heads down like children searching for a coin they had dropped, they kept themselves to themselves. And, of course, I had to get used to sleeping under covers. In the heat of the Caribbean you would sweat so much it would be impossible to sleep. Here, where the cold hovered about the room with icy intent. Not to dive under the three or four layers would have been madness!

There was a further surprise in store when I went to take a bath, my first. Eager to test the inviting porcelain I remember turning on the tap and sitting there, clutching the soap ready to enjoy the water caressing my body. I might have whistled as they do in movies, I might have hummed in anticipation of the warm gush. Then, like someone who has sat on a needle, up I shot when the water hit my toes and calves. It was cold, freezing cold! There would be so much to learn about England.

CHAPTER FOUR

Work

IT'S NOT UNCOMMON NOW TO walk past a house with three cars parked in the drive, and, unless you watch old television series or films, it's easy to believe that things have always been like this. Now that our houses are warmed or cooled to suit our taste, winter is no longer the grind or fear it once was. When we wake up each room is pleasingly warm, a drop-in temperature and we tweak the thermostat or thumb the dial. But few people could afford these luxuries in the 60s or 70s, I can't think of a single one. We had to rely on paraffin heaters for heat or to keep off the chill of the evening. Tall grey or green dalek-like contraptions, they stood like sentries in the middle of every room and puffed their smoke and heat to all corners.

They might seem like a relic from the dark ages, but the daleks were our salvation during the autumns and winters of those early years in England. Lethal things they were, although we didn't think so at the time. Every house had at least one, the inhabitants huddling round it to warm tingling fingers and frozen feet. The smoke got up your nostrils, the smell lodged in your clothes, even your underwear couldn't escape the paraffin stench.

I once caught my nightie on a heater and leapt into the air screaming with fright. I was about to be set alight! I was convinced my time had come, I thought, goodbye everyone, what a way to go! Dreadful, horrible things. Every now and again the news reported a fire from a heater left on overnight, or a death from one accidentally knocked over. But never locally, thank goodness, though I'm not sure that's the right thing to say. I have recently been told of a young man from Luton known as Man a Man, who died tragically in England in 1963. The story told is that he came home from work tired and lit his paraffin heater and fell asleep. The next morning, he was found in a room full of black smoke. He was 21. I look back on those days with a sense of dread, thankful that times have moved on, and pray for those people worldwide who still use them to heat their home.

I was 15 when I arrived in England, the heat of the sun still coursing through my young veins. I wasn't going to let the cold get the better of me, I was a fighter. After years of silence where I lived with my aunt. I wanted to open my lungs and shout until my throat throbbed from the effort. I wanted to get out there and do things, to see the places whose names sounded quaint and ancient, to throw off the shadow that had been slowly stifling me. It might be cold outside, but once the room was warm when I got home, life didn't seem that bad.

When I left SVG I had been in my final year at my school. My hope was to continue my education in England, but that wasn't to be. You could leave school at 14 or 15. I soon found out it was possible to learn a trade, to sign up as an apprentice. Jobs were plentiful and there were lots of small businesses locally. Bus travel was cheap and reliable. The wages weren't great but you had the choice of being a florist or seamstress or nurse or shop assistant. Given all these, I didn't mind going to work instead of picking up where I had left off at school. A job meant freedom and money, and I was determined to pay my way, assisting Mom to send for my younger siblings.

My first job was at a laundry shop. It's still there, I believe, I doubt that the owners know or care about the part it played in my story. Who got me the job I don't know. I imagine that it came through a friend of a friend or by word of mouth, that's how things were in those days. No page after page of application, no strenuous interviews. What is fresh in my memory though is the journey to work. I would walk for miles to the bus station in town, catch the first bus and then take a second bus to the place where the laundry shop it. I was becoming independent, I suppose, I was finding my feet if you can call it that, by planning my daily travel routine.

I suspect that I loved the journey to and from work more than the job itself. From the top of the bus I tried to identify the main landmarks I would eventually get to know and love: the rye with its eerie early morning mist, a beautiful park spread over its green acres. The job itself wasn't that demanding. Washing machines weren't commonplace so we had a stream of customers, many of them regulars. Between washes I got used to English accents, I laughed and grinned when I couldn't understand properly what the customers were saying.

The job was fairly easy to learn and quick to master. It was a matter of sorting fabrics and colours and following the manufacturers' instructions. The women who came regularly enjoyed a natter, it was a gentle introduction to the world of work. But, easy though it was, the chlorine-like smell gave me excruciating headaches and irritated my skin. At certain times during the year the sea in Georgetown in SVG seemed to be ill, giving off a salty rankness that made my stomach churn. It was the same feeling now at the launderette; sickly odours that got into my pores and made me want to throw up as soon as I entered the premises.

When the headaches became unbearable, I told my mother. I wasn't a quitter, she knew, so my condition had to be serious. She thought for a while then came up with a solution. She and most of the family worked at a rubber and plastics manufacturing company, why not try my luck there?

The company was situated a short distance from the town centre. It manufactured rubber and plastics and was one of the biggest employers of West Indians in the town. Other companies regulated the number of Caribbean people on their books – although they wouldn't have admitted it - but the company was happy to offer employment to anyone willing to work hard. If you were to talk to anyone in their 60s or older who lived in Fifth Street, there is a pretty good chance that they had a spell there: and if they hadn't then a relative or friend would have.

The wages were good, £10 per week went a long way in those days. The job involved piecework, with generous bonuses for the swiftest workers. Competition was fierce as you can well imagine. The older and more experienced women got the choice of cuts, in the scramble for these prime cuts serious rivalries often threatened the friendships carefully nurtured over many years.

I had no chance against these women. Most of them had been there 10 years or more, their trained eye could spot the easiest rubber sheets. I was slightly-built, my fingers were tender, I wasn't cut out for that kind of work. I saw the scars from years trimming coarse rubber on my mother's fingers, they were corned and calloused but she didn't complain. The black rings about the eyes from exposure to the rubber identified her as one of those who worked at the plant. She had an inkling that the nature of the job might be a threat to their health, but what could she or any of the other semi-skilled workers do? They were grateful for the job so why make a fuss? Yet the moment she came home from work she would insist on eating a little sugar to 'take away the taste of rubber'. Thankfully, I was quickly transferred to plastics, which was cleaner and less demanding and saved from ruined fingers and eyes.

Being young and ignorant of the possibilities England offered, I was happy to take the first job that came along. Educational opportunities were something few considered, even those who had quite high levels of schooling in the Caribbean were content to drop into a job that meant the security and regularity of a wage. So, although, looking back now, I wonder where else I might have gone had my mother not suggested joining her, I can well understand her willingness to place me in an environment with other West Indians where I would be comfortable.

In the rubber department at the company as well as in plastics, the factory supervisors seemed to take to me. I was small and frail, far younger than most of the workers, I suppose they saw in me something of their own children. 'Are you sure this is your daughter?' they teased my mother in the British way that took some getting used to. 'Are you sure it's not the milkman's?' Hands on our sides, me and mom would laugh uproariously at these early attempts to forge a relationship with people who knew as little of us as we knew about them.

One supervisor in particular used to send me on errands into the town centre, I remember, and I preferred this to working with plastics. Instead of sitting there wrestling to seal the rear light bulbs for cars into the plastic container, I would gladly set out to buy shampoo for her, or creams, or whatever she fancied! The longer the shopping list, the better. When I had found what she wanted I would spend the rest of the time window-shopping, or chatting to those who could spare the time.

Not a bad morning's work I would say to myself, if it happened to be a morning when the need for her products hit her. Especially if it meant returning just in time for lunch in the subsidized canteen many local companies at the time operated. Here, in between the teasing and flirting and loud conversations, I learned to scoff bangers, bacon and mash. I would watch with a wry smile as my fellow West Indians took to English food as if they had grown up with it. And yes, I was quick to join them, wolfing down apple crumble and custard like there was no tomorrow. Baked beans were the only things I couldn't stomach. How others devoured the wretched things I could never understand. How could beans ever be sweet, where did the sweetness come from?

With the benefit of hindsight, it occurred to me, it didn't take as long to settle into life in Fifth Street as I had feared it would when I first landed, but the early years have merged with the passing of time. They were what I regard as the phase of exploration and discovery. I was finding my feet, I was striving to work out what England was about. I grew to accept the bite of winter, light fluffy snow was as unreal then as it is romantic to me now. I was young, after all, I welcomed newness and adventure, and England promised them in abundance.

One of my sisters was my companion and guide during this phase of finding out about me and adapting to an English way of life. My elder sister had her family, so my younger sister took me under her wings. She led me to the places she loved, we went shopping together, and she introduced me to her multitude of friends. I was taught how to spot the people to avoid, warned in no uncertain terms to keep away from the gossipers. I got to learn the geography of the town, I found out where the people who would later become lifelong friends lived.

Under my sister's guidance I learned to dress with more sophistication, I discovered the styles that suited me and which to avoid like the plague. She widened my circle beyond the family, I was 'English' now she said, tongue-in-cheek.

It's impossible to write about the 60s in Fifth Street without a mixture of nostalgia and wonder. The wonder of a 16-year old, the nostalgia of a woman, let's call it well over 21. It was a different world indeed, but in many ways a better one, in my view.

The Caribbean community was smaller then, of course, but it seemed to me tighter than it is today. Perhaps the size led inevitably to the desire to look out for each other. People visited each other every Sunday, you wouldn't dream of not calling on someone you had heard was ill.

There were trips to the seaside, I can't recall anything like the spate of funerals we have been having recently. Newcomers were welcomed into rooms that were already overcrowded; it wasn't unusual to find someone asleep on your floor after a late-night event.

Many of the adults had lodged in the same hostels; the camaraderie of those times was tangible in all they said or did. Disagreements couldn't separate them, their children married to strengthen the ties. But I mustn't suggest that things were easy. We had it as hard then as we do now. Most West Indians rented properties, the banks refused to lend us money to buy the houses we had spent years renting. They saw us as a risk, that was their pathetic defense. On any given day there were skirmishes with teddy-boys and skinheads, the police too had their fun at our expense. Landlords could refuse you a room on a whim, a dozen obstacles could spring up in the course of a single Saturday for a West Indian seeking to establish a family in Fifth Street.

But we were never going to be defeated. Not by teddy-boys, skinheads or the law. We had inextricable links with England; senior ministers had personally invited us to the Mother Country to help out after the war. Even those who said disparaging things about us knew they couldn't accuse us of lacking fight. They chuckled that winter would find us out, that the cold of December and January would send us scurrying for the next plane 'home to the Caribbean sunshine'. These were probably the same people who were snug in their beds while we were trudging to the hospitals to care for our patients or driving the early buses in the fog, six layers of clothes piled on our backs, and two pairs of gloves. It would have required some catastrophe to repel our presence. I knew even then we have fight, we West Indians have spirit. I prefer not to dwell on the seamier side of these incidents because in my mind there was never any doubt that I was here to stay. I would leave when I was ready. And on my terms.

We pulled together then as West Indians during these testing times. We got to know our Caribbean neighbours; we could tease one another knowing that we were mocking ourselves and that no offence would be taken. I giggled at the way Jamaicans talked, I stood open-mouthed when I heard rich Bajan accents where you might only catch one word out of every three if you were lucky. We had our inter-island rivalries but these didn't prevent us seeking each other out. I tasted ackee for the first time, I heard Jamaicans speak and wondered if Jamaica was truly part of the Caribbean.

Finally, then, after two years in England watching and observing closely, I was ready to venture into the wider world. Caribbean people from the different islands were meeting for the first time, swapping music, dance, and tasting each other's rich dishes, how could I be left out?

When I was growing up, every weekend there seemed to be a dance, party or christening. Only fools waited to be invited. The bigger the crowd the better, that was the rule. Rooms creaked under strain of 60 people in a space designed for five, we were often so close you could only dance with a neighbour. There were dances at Marsh Lane opposite the church, the hall at Loudwater (now demolished) rocked and vibrated when they turned up the music, I was told. The Hall was a favourite venue, and occasionally the Town Hall. I had to get some of that action: I couldn't live on the stories others fed me, I had to taste the food myself.

Bands travelled from Oxford, London, Reading and Luton to play; the local band groups did the town proud. The new band was created and would appear on the popular national television programme for several weeks. It was a time of fun and laughter, only the old and tired stayed in to watch the two television channels we had at the time, BBC and ITV.

Music flooded this phase of my life. At home on a Saturday or Sunday we cleaned and tidied up to Jim Reeves or some other country and western artist, or the silky Nat King Cole. When we went out there was American soul, booming reggae and of course, spicy calypso. Slow or fast I danced and danced. Sometimes my feet would hurt from some late jaunt but what did I care? I was practising for life, fun and enjoyment were all that mattered to the teenage me. The harder the week at the company, the greater was the need to dance. I was young after all, single, without a care in the world, what was I expected to do?

I found that I could pick up a dance quickly, could hear where the singer was going, and whether or not the band was in tune with him or her. I paid close attention and the music was 10 times sweeter when I experienced the delicate harmony of music and voice.

I was learning about music but I was learning also the ways of men. Their wiles, their smiles, the ease with which they spun a yarn. As a young woman new on the scene, it didn't take long to spot the heads turning in my direction for a second look when I went by, or to observe the men inching in my direction with every song, waiting for the right combination of song and mood so that he could have a slow dance with me. It was funny to begin with, observing a man preparing to make a move on me or some other unsuspecting woman. He would shuffle to within a few metres, dance a couple of steps on his own, and eye you up discreetly. A few bars into the slow record he loved, before you could grasp what was happening, he would be asking for your hand, and you would be so close air couldn't separate you.

I learned to drink around this time too – cherry B, snowball and babycham –and to recognise my limit. One of my most important discoveries, and one that I cherished, was that if you were dancing with a man and he was contemplating a second dance – or a third - he would offer to buy you a drink. 'Cherry B, please,' I would say with an innocently grin if he was a good dancer or if I fancied him. 'Babycham and brandy,' I would suggest with a wide grin, if I wanted to put him to the test: men who thought a Babycham and brandy were too expensive never came back for a second dance!

Every West Indian in the town seemed to be at one of these dances, christenings or parties, at one stage or another. There were no tricky situations about invitations. If I found out about an event last minute I bathed, climbed into my dress and made a dash for it. The host with a sour face was a rarity, to turn away someone who had travelled from Luton or Oxford would have been the height of rudeness. Late invitation or early, Mom always insisted on going too. I was growing up, and I soon sussed that she dragged her tired body along to keep an eye on me. When I turned 18, I thought to myself, no, DD girl, this has to stop. You're too old for an escort, time to flex your muscles: you can't go around with your mother in the shadows like a 'macko' (someone watching you). Other girls went out on their own, they stayed late, was there anything more frustrating than having to leave a function before the end and discover that I had missed the grand finale? Once I became of age, I didn't ask Mom, I simply told her I was going out my brother.

What wonderful times! The Nags Head, The Angel, The Red Cross Knight, what delicious memories! Pubs welcomed people from all musical backgrounds, we didn't waste our youth, it was almost heaven. Stumbling home at three in the morning, high on music, drafting off to sleep with the events of the night replaying in my head like a loop of my favourite film; I didn't want these days and nights to end.

There was a piano at a place I use to go before, a beaten-up old instrument with several keys missing. We used to joke that it needed to see the dentist. My brother used to play the piano, teasing out tunes that were surprisingly melodic considering the age and battered state of the instrument. He had made banjos in SVG, he had a gift for music and now, one evening, as he was tinkering away he turned to me and said, 'Come on DD, come sing for me.' I was a bit hesitant to begin with. Me, sing? And to the accompaniment of a decrepit off-key piano? No way. But with a little brotherly persuasion, I was soon Gladys Knight or Aretha Franklin, with her unsurpassable vocals, my hands flung out in a grand theatrical gesture, as if I was top billing at The London Palladium.

My brother was amazed. I can still picture his face now, the small eyes widening, the eyebrows rising, the glow of pleasure spreading across his face. 'Oh my God, DD,' he gurgled, cocking his head to the right, 'what a wonderful voice you have! One of these days we must form a group.' I didn't take him seriously it was just a bit of fun for me, something you would do to pass a Sunday evening that was dragging along. He had asked me to sing and I had joined him, nothing more, nothing less. So my voice was good, but what of it? My brother didn't give up easily, though. As far as he was concerned my voice was more than good: it possessed a quality that demanded to be heard. From then on wherever there was a dance we would gate-crash it and ask to perform.

Those were the days when it wasn't considered bold or barefaced for a musician to do such a thing: ask to play at an event and be granted a slot. Nowadays there would be haggling about money, health and safety considerations, insurance to worry about. My brother was daring and he was well known, so getting onto the bill wasn't as difficult as might be imagined. I

don't remember us rehearsing or doing any serious practice for these events; we simply went along, asked if a slot was available, and if there was, we sang then went back into the crowd to enjoy ourselves for the remainder of the event.

A former policeman was a prominent member of one of local Caribbean organisations in the town. In SVG he wasn't one to miss a social. I remember his reaction at one of these early functions. In my mind I can still see him standing there, open-mouthed as I began a number, probably an Aretha Franklin cover. Later, when my songs appeared in the charts he would confirm that he first heard me sing in public at Loudwater Village Hall. I was quite young, and I was 'doing a duet with a chap called Buddy', he told the local newspaper. According to his account the audience thought that the duet was the showpiece of the evening.

My brother, he would say what he thought I wanted to hear. But my neighbour? Who had only seen me shopping in town with my Mom? Perhaps I did have a voice after all.

CHAPTER FIVE

The Band

MY BROTHER TINKLING WITH A piano on its last legs, the high notes metallic, the low ones as hollow as a grumbling stomach; I can recall the look of amazement on my brother's face that evening when he first heard my singing voice. At his suggestion I had joined him in a duet, and somehow the sound we created had truly impressed him, a natural musician if ever there was one. If his sister had a talent for singing he had to do something about it, I could tell that this was going through his mind from the expression on his face. The thoughtful look and quiet delight in his eyes couldn't help but develop into a broad smile.

My brother mixed regularly with those who had an ear for music. He played in several bands, from reggae to calypso to soul and pop. Sister or no sister, if he thought I was a pretender whose voice would break under the strain of a song he would have said so. There was his reputation to uphold. For what good is it stringing along a young hopeful and have her embarrass herself in public and drag him down at the same time? Perhaps he had dreamt about forming his own band but had never followed through with the idea. Now, though, finally, in his mind, and right in his home, I could tell that he could see possibilities.

What happened next happened quite quickly. So swiftly that I was swept along with it like the branch of a tree rushed downstream by a swollen river. My brother must have been very persuasive with me if not the others he occasionally jammed with. My experience had been limited to singing along to the songs on the radio, or during a long hot bath, so I must have taken some convincing. Me appear onstage and putting myself at the mercy of people screaming for tough reggae, sweet soul and deadly calypso to dance to? Yes, I was able to appreciate the harmony of a church choir, yes I could tell intuitively when a singer had grasped a song and wrung every ounce of feeling from it, but the idea of fronting a band? The thought had never crossed my mind. Yet, not long after brothers' brotherly compliment, my first band had taken shape.

My brother was responsible for the name that would get us known in Fifth Street and the surrounding towns in the late 60s and 70s. He might have been thinking of the name for a while, it could well have been a flash of daring. Why not, I imagine thinking, why not make a play of a band with our name? However, he came by the name, for 10 years or so, my first band would play venues across the country, entertaining thousands of fans, Caribbean as well as English.

So my brother was the mastermind, the person responsible for my introduction into the world of music and performing. Without these early groundings, would I have had the confidence to contemplate a recording career? How can I ever repay him? How could I thank him for insisting that I have a go at the piano? Ever full of energy and drive he sought out people of ability, recruiting those with similar ambitions.

The humblest band requires hours of practice and rehearsals so he was careful in selecting those who were prepared to make the necessary sacrifices. Anyone who couldn't fully commit to the group he waved away. He had no intention in putting together a unit that bubbled for six months then fizzled out. Equipment didn't come cheap, costumes could set you back 20 pounds, time was too precious to squander. From the beginning he made sure that we took ourselves seriously, that we knew what we had signed up for. Too many groups had folded within months of forming. Without discipline and commitment, he lectured us, like a teacher to her pupils on their first day at school, my first band would simply add to their number.

He was my brother, how could I let him down and the others who had readily accepted me, offering encouragement, giving me the benefit of their musical expertise? Who but a donkey-fool would have repaid their faith with sloppiness? I had never been that kind of person, I wasn't going to become one now. Each day I would race home from work, scoop down my supper and scramble for the bus to take me to rehearsal. Month after month, five days a week, I stuck to this demanding routine. Work, supper, bus, rehearsal, same again the following day. We met up nightly at a band mate's house and practiced for hours in his basement, sometimes well into the early hours of morning. When this was unavailable, some of my friends gladly opened their basement for the fledgling band. Cold and fog couldn't stop us; no band member was distracted by the pleasure of a hot sunny evening. Is it too late to acknowledge the role they played in my early career?

It was quite a large band. My band mates played the guitar, the drums, and my brother controlled the keyboard. Accompanied with two other men (which one of them would have a chart hit in August 1976) shared the singing. Our repertoire was mainly the American soul standards of the day, Otis Redding, Sam Cooke, Al Green, Aretha Franklin, and one my favourites, Ben E King. 'Stand by Me' we sang in our own Caribbean way, throwing our everything into our performance, toying with the audience but sending them home satisfied, 'please stand by me.' I modelled myself on Aretha Franklin, soulful, smoulderingly sexy. And yes, I don't mind admitting, I enjoyed lapping up the attention as the only female group member!

At the time, the idea of writing our own material never crossed our minds. To us signwriting belonged to the Americans whose slick profiles appeared on the record sleeves, or who strutted easily on the television screen as if they had been born to it. They were our heroes, glamorous, the epitome of sophistication. As we played for a wider circle I began to pay more and more attention to the performance of these soul stars, observing each gesture, making a mental note of their every movement. What I liked I incorporated into my performance and this was to pay off when I, too, hit the charts.

From the effortless poise of these superstars I then switched my attention to the wonderful dresses of the women. Their shoes must have cost a fortune I remember thinking, their hairstyles must have taken hours to perfect! I watched and listened and dreamt. Each performance was sprinkled with magic; their fame was beyond anything I would ever achieve, wasn't it? But once we did justice to their songs the band was satisfied; we did our best to entertain the crowds that paid their hard-earned cash to see us, that was all anyone could ask us. Our goal was to send them home to their cold or warm beds with love in their hearts. Any thoughts beyond that stayed in the heads of those who dared to dream.

The joy of performing to a large audience! How to describe that feeling? The crowd charged with expectation; the waves of heat pulsing through a hall; the perfume of hundreds of fans, sweat lighting up their faces in anticipation: how could we not respond?

Youth clubs, pubs, weddings or christenings, we were more than happy to oblige. The promoter who engaged us got full value for his money. We travelled to Oxford, Reading, Luton, Slough and London, wherever there was a Caribbean community they would get to see us. The nurses, bus drivers, electricians, plumbers, factory workers and domestics who were up at dawn every day, saving what they could of their wages to send for relatives but needing a weekly treat, flocked to see us. And we didn't let them down. How could we, when we too toiled away in our other lives outside the band?

At the time the by-laws weren't as restrictive as they are today. A band could play in a pub well into the early hours and only a few neighbours might complain about noise. Similarly for the town halls. These were affordable then and seen by many as the places to hire for a major event. Weddings and christenings drew hundreds and we played them all. From one town to another we were in demand, and I can't remember a single occasion when I came away feeling that we had been a disappointment.

It felt good to be recognized. I'm at the stage where I'm able to admit that recognition gives me a thrill. In and around town people would greet me and compliment the band on our performances. They encouraged, there was never a bad word. We had given the town something to be proud of, we were part of them, and they were happy to lend us their support. 'Last Saturday night was great,' they would say, 'where you playing this weekend?' Or, 'That song you closed with in Reading was fantastic, I'd love to hear it again.' I was what the local paper would call a 'factory girl' years later when I was in the charts, but at the time I could feel the lure of music gently tugging at my sleeve. Would I be able to resist?

What is there to trump a night of hot music and sweet dancing? Just imagine the mood in a noisy hall, the stage empty but for the cold instruments. Then suddenly the lights blaze and there is a hush of anticipation. For an instant you can hear your own breathing. In the time it takes to tie your shoe laces music is flooding the room and people are dancing as though they've been switched from Off to On. To witness an audience taking to the music, dancing singly or as couples as if they couldn't bear for the evening to end, is one of the things I've enjoyed most about my 'work', if indeed I can call making music work.

My brother had put together a professional unit and our popularity soared. I learned to sing in cold venues and warm, in front of hundreds or tens. It was all part of my apprenticeship, I suppose, and every singer needs this initiation. Our agent got us gigs outside our own circles, I remember that we even played in faraway Dorset. When the town halls were busy the Nags Head or some other pub was happy to have us.

So we played far and wide, there was hardly a weekend when we weren't on the road. But we didn't make much money. A large band, a van to transport instruments and equipment, there was never going to be a large pot to share after even the most lucrative event. But we weren't doing it to make our fortunes, music was in our blood, we would have almost performed just for the love of it.

All the band members loved to dress for a show but my brother was the most flamboyant of us all. He couldn't resist outlandish colours and styles and he knew the places to go to get the look no one else in our community could sport. He had the advantage of several years in England before me, he also had the advantage of being a man. He would take me to the different towns and some of his other haunts, and we would try out the latest fashions. Stilettoes, clogs, miniskirts, flowing dresses, I felt as glamorous as the stars we sometimes glimpsed on our shopping jaunts: I wanted to be more than the factory girl working in the plastics department before.

And at weekends, among the hopefuls and curious on the London scene I could be exactly that. Just observing people who were bursting with energy and ideas, who created music and fashion, who thought nothing of getting up and dancing if the mood struck them, was to enter into a world millions of miles away from my humdrum one. This was truly an eye-opening experience for me. We bumped into other singers and musicians in the West End, we got to see and hear live English music. My brother would try out the guitars and keyboards in the music shops searching for the perfect sound. I remember that he was very fond of the Hammond organ. After a gruelling day in London we returned to Fifth Street decked out in the latest fashions, seeing ourselves as trendsetters. I sensed that I might have a life with music in it, but at the time I had no idea of the scale or the pain it would involve.

I was young, fit, attractive, I began to be noticed in the town and at the venues we played. But now the compliments became more personal, detached from the band. Caribbean men would meet me in the street and said they loved me, I learned to smile but keep my gaze right ahead. My sister, who had taken me under wings since my arrival in England, was my companion at the time. She was single, so we went to most places together. I suppose she saw it as her responsibility to look after me, still a relative newcomer to England. 'Tell him to go and take a running jump,' she would suggest when a man was coming too strong, 'don't smile back, or he'll think you're interested.' If he was persistent, or crude, she would find the right phrase for me to pass on to him, although I could never bring myself to say it.

I remember once walking along the rye with my sister when this man said to me, 'I'm coming to see your mom.' I burst out laughing for I had never heard anything so ridiculous. I knew him only by sight, we didn't have any kind of relationship, what was he going to say when my mother asked him why he had come knocking at her door? 'Tell him to get lost,' I remember my sister saying, or words to that effect but a lot riper. But being slightly naive, I just shrugged my shoulders: could this man really be that doltish? When I got in mom was waiting with a very stern look on her face. What was I doing cavorting with some foolish old man, she asked? That was exactly what he was, I explained to her, a foolish old man I wouldn't even give the time of day. But even after my version of events my mother wasn't amused: but then which mother is?

Yet others came. Local men, mostly, but I distinctly remember one driving all the way from Luton. I had to hand it to him for sheer cheek: anyone prepared to drive 30 miles to present his credentials for a woman he might only have said 'Hello' to at a show deserved a special award, although I don't know for what.

The most remarkable of my 'visitors' was an African man, I'm not sure which country he was from, probably Nigeria or possibly Ghana. I had enrolled on a secretarial course at the college and Francis used to wait by the gate for me in the evenings. I wasn't interested, I told him, I simply wanted to be left alone to get on with my studies. He wouldn't accept this. He then took to buying me gifts which he would deliver to our house. For some reason I've never been able to discover, Mom would accept the presents (they were jewellery mainly) but I wouldn't touch them. I was afraid he might have put voodoo in them! But he wouldn't give up. When he persisted in hanging about waiting for me at the college gate I gave up the course.

CHAPTER SIX

Daughter

THERE WAS ONE MAN I fancied at the time, no point in denying it. Locksley, everyone called him. He played in the band also and had a wonderful singing voice. It was a measure of the quality of the band that he too had a top 10 hit in the British charts. The BBC clip on You Tube from 1976 shows him decked out in the most enormous flares, accentuating the slim, toned physique I secretly admired.

When the band was at its peak Locksley would find himself at our house and my heart would thump away whenever I heard the familiar voice at the door. He came mainly on Saturday mornings. After a deep hug we would laugh and joke and he would make himself comfortable. If I had on home clothes I would think of changing into something more appealing; if I was decent I would rue not doing my hair or not putting on a little perfume. I liked to look my best, which woman doesn't?

We would talk about the band, a recent gig, the weather, anything that came into our minds. In the background I would hear mom working away and occasionally the gorgeous aroma of her Caribbean stews would waft its way to us. A couple of drinks later and Locksley would do justice to mom's pea soup or roast. If the room was hot or he particularly enjoyed the meal he might take a short nap. But, not long after he would be on his way. How long did this sequence of knock at the door, girlish excitement, a hot meal, goodbye, last? I'm not exactly sure. 'Today's the day,' I told myself each time, 'he will pluck up the courage and ask mom's permission to take me out.' But it wasn't a matter of courage. Eventually I realized that our weekend visitor wasn't coming to see me:

mom's cooking was what he was after: to him, I discovered later, I was just a little girl! When I realized this, I wasn't despondent. It was probably just a girlish fantasy I consoled myself, just as well I hadn't made a fool of myself. Besides, I could still turn heads and the promises to call home for me hadn't dried up.

The men who came knocking at the house flattered and embarrassed me at the same time. I had never gotten beyond a cheerful 'Hello' with a single one of them, where they got the idea that I might be interested puzzled me with every new potential suitor. Some women might have been all 'hot up' by their attempt to blackmail me into going out with them by ingratiating themselves with Mom, but I took their behaviour in my stride. If a man wanted to make an ass of himself why stop him? One man, though, had caught my interest, but coming home for a woman wasn't his style, as I was to discover.

He was short, probably about five-six, handsome, solidly-built, with powerful square shoulders. There was a 'coolness' to him, he was suave, dapper. Where did this easy charm come from? It was probably due to the quiet self-confidence some short men seem able to conjure up; he bore his height with the uprightness of a six-footer.

He used to pick me up after work in his sports car and he had the words to impress an inexperienced 19-year old. For although I had gotten used to being chatted up or told how much a man desired me, I had never truly listened to what a man spouted. This time things we different, the words came, I listened, and quickly fell under his spell. We would meet up in secret, in a pub, under the cover of the darkness in a club, he was as charming as could be. It didn't take long to discover another aspect to myself: a deliriously happy one, full of sweet dreams and wild longings.

I was a young woman; new feelings were stirring within me. My body ached now, it developed a tenderness to touch I hadn't felt before. The music I played with the band excited lovers, sent them home with the joy of anticipation in their hearts. At some point someone else's music was bound to have the same effect on me.

I fell pregnant. The day I missed my period I was certain of it. Pregnancy-kit confirmation and all that paraphernalia weren't necessary, my young body told me all I needed to know.

I didn't know what to do. Not in the days immediately following the discovery, not in the weeks that added their voice to my new condition. I was gripped by panic. You hear of people having the rug pulled from under their feet and it was the same terrifying sensation with me. I stumbled from place to place as if I had lost my balance; my head felt light, I was dizzy with uncertainty. My work, the band and my home life could no longer provide the support or the distraction I needed, I was in a state. My world had crashed, for weeks I must have walked around as if in a daze.

Mom had such high hopes for me, I chided myself, Caribbean mothers pray that their children would seize the opportunities they didn't have. They are protective of their daughters, they try to shield them from the wily rascals who roam the town. Of course Mom wanted me to experience the joy of becoming a mother but certainly not like this. I was an ordinary young woman and although I hadn't given the future much thought, that wasn't how I had seen it unfolding. Like my friends I had visions of myself walking down the aisle one day, a loving husband by my side, with children following a couple of years down the line. What had I done, I asked myself repeatedly when the news struck home, what was going to happen to me now?

The man I had the 'liaison' with, for that is the word I now use to describe our relationship, was popular, but I was too young to know that and to fully appreciate what might be in store. We enjoyed being together, at least I thoroughly enjoyed being with him. I couldn't see beyond our hugging and kissing and slow dancing in the low lights of a smoky club. We were young, after all, and young people do young people things. Where parents attempt to shadow their children every waking minute they stifle their growth, risk ruining their lives.

When I gave him the news he appeared shocked, stunned, as if he had never been close to me. 'Let's get married', 'Let's set up together', 'We'll bring up the child together': I don't know what I was expecting him to say if indeed I was expecting anything, but he didn't respond with anything like the above as other men might have out of nervousness or a sense of duty. But he was the father and I had told myself that he had a right to know. But in telling him I felt there was a cold relegation of our relationship to indifferent depths.

I did not see him as often anymore. There was no car waiting for me outside the factory gate now, I had to trudge home after work with my guilty secret. And the secret soon became a burden. Paranoia even, the feeling that others could see through me, that they knew the facts I was desperately trying to conceal. The journey seemed longer each day, I drifted past familiar buildings without properly seeing them, I smiled and waved to acquaintances then walked sullenly on.

It was a lonely, unsettling time for me. Other young women had fallen to early pregnancy but in my mind, I had nothing in common with them. Mine was just one of those things. What really brought home to me the gravity of the situation was the fact that now I saw the man who months earlier was whispering to me that there was no one else, driving around town with other women in his sports car. In the very seat I used to occupy two or three others now sat and felt the wind in their faces as he sped along.

These first few months were long and traumatic for me. From the time I found out to the news truly sinking in. Blame isn't something I go in for, it doesn't get you very far, I've found, and we can't undo what has been done. So I didn't chastise myself, and I didn't blame the man. For what was the point? We were roughly the same age, wasn't what we did the most natural thing in the world?

Consequences never once entered our young minds, at least not mine. Together we lived for the sweet moments, we shut out the rest of the world, I had to accept the payment.

Still, I was shocked that his reaction had not been to join with me and support me and stick by me so we could go through it together. What I saw as the ease and casualness with which he brushed our relationship aside, was what hurt most. Not once did he ask how I felt, no sympathetic hug. I would have been buoyed by even some pretence that he truly cared for me and would be there to lend his support. Our relationship had been vigorous and physical but, even so, I had expected some understanding of what I might be going through, some recognition that our lives were about to link inextricably. 'We're in this together,' he could have lied: but it began to dawn on me that I would not be hearing any of those words.

He drifted out of my life, easily, causally, like a high rain cloud with its promise to cool the land. I can say for sure I was not asked if I had told my mother, there were no promises to care for me and the baby, I was angry and upset then but now I see things differently. I learned that a bird will go from tree to tree pecking at the sweet mangoes as it is easily tempted by yellower, juicier fruit. But I won't lie, it was extremely painful to be dismissed so readily, to be casually brushed off like a hair on a jacket. There was no explanation. Maybe if I was made to understand why what I thought was a solid relationship had crumbled so suddenly, and at this particular time, it would have been easier to bear. But it was a life lesson I had to learn.

With each passing week I grew more and more desperate. It took me a while to recover my self-esteem. How was I going to face my mother after I had given her the news? Every time we were alone, I searched for the words but they wouldn't come out. I watched her closely, judged her mood, yet when it came to uttering the fateful words my courage failed me. For what could I say? How could I put the fact that I was pregnant and that there was no prospect of a marriage to the father, without hurting her? How would she take the news? Every woman wants a better life than the one she had been dealt for her daughter. Would she spring at me in anger, curse me, would she cry and hang her head in shame?

I prayed that no one would suspect and whisper their suspicions to her. And I recently discovered something that sent shivers down my spine. It wasn't unusual in the 70s and 80s for members of one band in the town to play for another local one. In fact, some musicians from our town chopped and changed so frequently it was like having dual membership, if I could call it that. I myself sometimes sang for these bands when they were in need of a lead singer.

At a recent get-together at an elderly care center, two former members of a band in town brought to my attention an incident I swear I can't remember. Apparently, I was singing for a band and they both noticed that I wasn't on form that night. 'DD is singing like she is ill,' one whispered to the other. 'She must be pregnant,' the other replied casually, not knowing the bitter truth. They both had a clear recollection of the conversation that night. I dread to think what might have happened if they had passed on their suspicions to their friends and the news had got to Mom that way.

I couldn't face telling Mom directly, and the longer I waited the worse it got. Soon I would begin to show and I couldn't stand the thought of her noticing before I broke the news. Still worse was the thought that some other woman with 'intuition' might get an inkling and confront her with their suspicion. Even thinking about that possibility made me shiver. Yet I couldn't pluck up the courage to face her. So one day I left her a note. Left it in the room where she could find it.

Mom was pragmatic, that's the only way I can describe her reaction. If she was angry inside she didn't show it. There might have been a sad weary sigh but I can't remember it. I watched her closely, my whole being on edge, ashamed but relieved that she now knew what had been tormenting me for months. After the shock of the message of the note she was calm, decisive. You're not going to be on your own, Mom made that clear at once. She would support me, the entire family would be there for me every step of the way. Mothers, oh mothers, where do they find the strength?

But our accommodation in town could just about take us, she pointed out, finding room for a young baby was going to be a challenge. Having accepted my condition, I could see her trying to work out the little details in her mind in the ensuing weeks. 'Children are a gift, DD,' I could imagine her saying when the news had properly sunk in; 'despite the predicament we get ourselves into, bringing forth a child remains the miracle of all miracles.'

With my mind a bit clearer and knowing that my family was going to be there for me, I became more settled. Settled enough, that is, to ward off panic. I had good days, then at other times I felt utterly miserable. Up and down swung my moods without rhyme, without reason. I didn't suffer from morning sickness and the outlandish cravings some women develop passed me by. What I did experience were extreme highs and desperate lows, spells of joy quickly dampened by feelings of helplessness. That they were beyond my control didn't lessen their impact on me. They sapped my energy, took me to depths I wouldn't wish on anyone.

One day I decided to visit the mother of my child's father. I might have been planning to all along, the thought might have suddenly come to me; my memories of how I arrived at the decision are hazy.

She was a short, squat woman and she worked at the company also. Her son might have already given her the news, I didn't really think of that. Some impulse drove me to go and see her and so that day off I trekked. Whether or not he had told her, she was a woman, she would understand my anxiety, wouldn't she? Women have this bond, don't they? I was young, a fist time mother-to-be, she would have the comforting words I needed, wouldn't she?

We might have had a cup of tea that morning, digestives or a slice of cake might have been offered to the unexpected visitor. In the quiet of the living room we might even have made small talk, but the memory of that meeting was hazy except for the words that kept ringing in my head thereafter: 'If you have sex you have to protect yourself.' Could these cold callous words have come from a prospective grandmother? Was that her response after I broke the news? All I recall is that I had the most chilling and deflating feeling of my young life after that meeting.

I had dreaded telling my mother, and now I felt like I had been dismissed in the most stinging manner imaginable when all I had sought was a word or two of comfort from the grandmother of my child, Was this just one of my extreme mood swings that left me feeling desperately low? After all, she was a woman, I had told myself on the way there, she would understand, she would offer a sympathetic shoulder. I didn't believe I had done anything to arouse her contempt, but I couldn't help wondering, who she thought I was. I was in a state when I left the house. My head was spinning, I might have cried, and I cannot recall where I went directly afterwards or what I did.

The success of the band meant that I was well known in the town. In a small community this recognition gave me a quiet sense of pleasure, I have to admit. It gave me a thrill to be recognised. People looked forward to our performances as the 'front' of my first band. I was aware that the band was seen as 'belonging' to the community. What would people in the community say now that I was pregnant and when they found out who the father was? I felt as if I had let them down. Not simply those who came to every show, but those who backed us when our detractors piped up. No matter how hard I tried I couldn't shake off the feeling that I had lost the respect of the community.

Despite her kind words of reassurance and her ready acceptance of my plight,

I sometimes wondered if Mom felt a tinge of disappointment with what I had done. 'You should have known better,' I imagined her holding back from saying to me, 'I sent for you from St Vincent, I brought you up properly, you're too young to become a mother.' The battle raged within me, up and down swung my moods.

Eventually I delivered a beautiful baby girl. Every new mother says it, but delivery was the most marvelous experience. The labour that seemed as though it would never end, the cajoling of the midwife and nurses, the pain, it was all truly worth it just to see her pretty face; and to know her complete dependence on me created a bond only mothers could ever know. Lively, alert, pretty, I was mother to a gorgeous infant! I felt as proud of myself as my family were of me.

But after the warm comforting glow of becoming a mother came the harsh reality: the nappies (diapers), the sleepless nights, the crying and wailing, feeding, the fevers and chills. No amount of preparation ever prepares you for it. Adjustments have to be made, you adapt or fail abjectly. My baby took over my life, how else could I put it?

But work hadn't gone away. The world waits for no one, they say, it continues to spin whether we like it or not. There were bills to pay, I was a single mother, I had to earn a living, but for two now, not just myself. My sister had married and moved by this time, and she looked after my baby while I went to work. I can still picture myself trekking from our neighborhood, then past the railway station. Finally, after a slight downhill, I would push the pram up the steep gradient of a small town on a hill, turning right at the top, then right again, resting when I reached the flat stretch of road. A 1400cc car might have to shift to second gear to take the same hill today, with a pram in the 70s the effort was back-breaking. But it had to be done. There was some slight compensation, though, if I could call it that: the rush back to work at the company was downhill!

My family had stood by me and now others came forward. Instead of the tut-tutting and shaking of heads, well-wishers sprang up where I had least expected. My apprehensions evaporated, people accepted me as a mother. I particularly remember a neighbour from the company as one whose intuition told her that a young mother sometimes needs a hug. When I got depressed or moody she was always there to look after me. She brought me food, she reassured me that things would work out well in the end. My child was a blessing, she never let me forget, she was like a second mother. One of the supervisors was another stalwart, I remember. He laid a protective arm around my shoulders when I needed it, he lifted my spirits when he noticed me flagging.

They didn't chuck out mother and child from the maternity unit with the indecent haste of today's hospitals. We were allowed to rest after our labour and the infant to settle into the unfamiliar surroundings. I remember one of my guy friends' visiting me at the Shrubbery during his lunch break one day. This was typical of him, kind, thoughtful, considerate. When family members couldn't make it, I could guarantee that he would find his way there. He would ask how I was; he would update me on what was going on at work. But his visits had an unfortunate consequence. One of the Caribbean nurses gave me a terrible time as a result of these friendly gestures. I was young, only my family came to visit, I suppose this particular nurse took one and one and made five. 'Look upon you,' she sneered when he had returned to work. 'You and your white baby: you'll be back.' 'You'll have to wait a long time,' I answered. If she was closer and if I had the strength, I'm sure I would have slapped her.

During this time not a single member of my daughters' father's family came to visit. Not one. When she was born, even after what I called my encounter with her grandmother, I had expected a call or visitor even a card, something to acknowledge the addition to both our families. Her father would show up too, I had imagined, for which man doesn't feel proud of a beautiful daughter? It was a vain hope. Her father didn't make contact, my daughter was a Jack, their absence implied she was the responsibility of our family, not theirs.

Her dad was popular with women; his easy charm carried him a long way. He didn't attempt to hide his latest conquest. Some in the string of women he attracted knew each another well, I believe, but that didn't concern me now. Our lives had touched for one brief moment and what he did now was none of my concern.

One day I ran into the grandmother and had a flashback to the words "protect yourself". I didn't much care for her but nevertheless I tried to remain polite. Bring the baby round, she suggested, after we had exchanged greetings. I

laughed inside to myself as I watched the short rectangular-shaped woman whose presence I had left just months ago feeling so bad about myself; flipping cheek, I thought, hell would freeze over first!

When things returned to normal, I re-joined the band and picked up where I had left off as best I could.

And when the band played out now, for some perverse reason, my daughter's father seemed to be at every show. At a club in town, I could make him out in the audience staring at me and I was sure he always had a smug grin. What he was grinning about I could never understand. Was he trying to intimidate me? I certainly would not be foolish enough to waste my time trying to figure him out.

brought up my beautiful daughter, an accountant now and herself a mother of two, with the help of my family and our close friends, saw her through illnesses and school without as much as a card or a dress from anyone on her father's side. Her grandmother never made the short trip to our home for a visit.

My daughter wasn't to discover who her father was until she was 16. He met her in Fifth Street town centre one day, introduced himself and 'invited her for tea'. She came home all excited and confused. She had never asked about her father and I had never seen the need to broach the subject. What should she do, she now asked?

She was a high school student at the time, old enough to know the truth. We enjoyed a good relationship, I didn't keep anything from her I felt she had a right to know. I sat her down and explained the situation. 'Yes,' I said, 'yes, he is your father. If you want to go to tea with him, it's your decision.' She was old enough to understand, I had always intended to tell her about him when I felt she was ready for it. 'I won't go,' she said when I had finished my account, 'I don't need him.'

But her father was persistent if not with his daughter then certainly with me. He had his other women and children galore scattered about the town, but I got the impression that for some inexplicable reason he seemed to believe that I might still have feelings for him or he was the band's number one fan. At a show in London, who did I spot in the front row but him and his mother! And at a party in town, there he was again.

My daughter met a fair number of her many half-brothers and half-sisters, but we didn't see her father or hear from him after he migrated to Canada in the 80s.

CHAPTER SEVEN

Husband

OVER THE COURSE OF A set from the lofty advantage of the stage, a singer gets a keen sense of the audience. Even as you channel your energies into delivering a good performance you can observe the petit dramas gradually unfolding before you. In the dark corner to the right a couple might be 'hooked up', dancing slow and extremely close no matter what the tempo of the song; in the half-light on the left you might notice a man marking time, inching towards his target, an unsuspecting woman, waiting for a particular song, or perhaps double-checking that she is unattached in order to avoid a scuffle.

Bang in the centre, dancing wild and without care, a group of women (or men) invariably springs up, charging themselves for another week in a monotonous job, insulating themselves against the stresses outside the door. You can spot all these happening and feel satisfied that you are bringing some pleasure to the lives of those who have travelled miles to see the band. Waves of perfume and the heat of thrusting bodies and ripe alcohol waft up to the stage, and you know things are going well. When the music hits home and the dancing is sweet and subtle, there are few greater pleasures for a band or singer. And it was one such heady night of music and dancing and gaiety in Luton that was to change my life forever.

This was in 1972, two years after my daughter's birth. I was now an accepted young mother (was the term single mother around at the time?), and I had returned to work at the company. After the initial disorientation of motherhood, I felt settled again, the reins of my life firmly gathered in my hands. My daughter was a beautiful child, loved and cared for by family and friends alike,

she was no trouble to look after. There was no need to worry about her well-being, I could journey to a gig safe in the knowledge that Mom or another relative was in charge. That evening in Luton, then, I was well into the set when I noticed this man in the audience, dancing away near the front of the stage. He was tall, handsome and a good mover, and in between moves he would stare at me. What could I do but smile back? Which performer stands there on stage with a sour face?

During the interval he found me and we got talking. Up close he was even taller than he had seemed from the stage. He was a year younger than me, and he was from Guyana. Somewhere in conversation he asked for my number. He was bold as well as handsome, I remember thinking to myself. He had small almond-shaped eyes and soft, short black hair. It was a hot night with an appreciative audience, the buzz was tangible, it was the kind of night where you danced wild and ignored the consequences. So, in keeping with the mood of the evening, I scribbled the number on a piece of paper, handed it to him, and returned to the second half of our set. Within months we were seeing one another.

For almost two years I had deliberately avoided relationships. After the episode with my daughter's father I had no wish of a repeat performance. They say that motherhood makes a woman more attractive to men and, in my case that certainly seemed to be true. They loved me even more now, the number who wanted to take care of me was laughable. I easily brushed them aside, I was in no hurry to commit to someone who shrank from the words 'commitment' and 'responsibility'. But my mind told me that this man would be different. I wasn't wrong, but not in the way I had envisaged.

My husband made me feel special; he took me for who I was. And he had the air of mystery some men possess that you can't help wanting to probe to discover more about them. He came to see me, we went dancing and he was delightful company in a quirky kind of way. We had moved by then and I was saving up for a place of my own. I introduced him to Mom on one of his visits and was pleased to see how well they got on. In return he invited me to Luton to meet his mother and I found a lovely lady, genuine and welcoming. We soon realized that things were getting serious between us so by then we moved out.

He got a job in one of the most prestigious companies in the area. Not long after this we got married, and he moved into my tiny room. Things happened so quickly I'm astonished now at our haste. The momentum of the relationship had swept us both along once we had decided there was no turning back. And even though the living arrangements weren't ideal we made the most of them, and began married life like any other young Caribbean couple, full of hope and dreams.

My husband was a cricketer, a crafty spinner, in one of the established Caribbean clubs in the town. The team played in the local league on Saturdays and on Sundays there were friendly matches. Reading, Luton, London, he introduced me to what we still regard as our traditional Caribbean game. I got to enjoy the drama of a tight league match against a local English team, it was like discovering another world. I overheard players fuss over their kit, I watched them discuss tactics in the animated way the band argued over which songs suited our style. My summers were long and sun-filled, glorious days that seemed to stretch to midnight.

The league matches could get intense and acrimonious, so I truly looked forward to the friendly outings against other West Indian teams, Caribbean people from all walks of life. I got to see towns I had never been to, we even played against cricketing 11s on the south coast. If a squabble developed on the field my husband would be in the middle of it, arms slinging wildly like a disgruntled father hurling away the Christmas presents from his bulging sack. He had a quick temper, his team mates warned me, and I soon saw for myself that he would fly off the handle at the slightest provocation. I made a mental note of the fact, but I didn't let it worry me unduly.

The Caribbean Cricket Club was formidable, popular, with dozens of fans in Fifth Street prepared to give to give up their Saturdays or Sundays to watch a tight game of bat versus ball. It was a strong, successful team, confident, the fans were seldom disappointed with their fighting spirit. Wives and girlfriends went along to support, taking with them the children and babies. I grew to love the traditions of cricket during my early years with him.

The leisurely pace of the game allowing time for tea and conversation, fitted me perfectly. During a dull period of play I could read a newspaper, there were those who packed a magazine or a book for an afternoon under the bright sunshine. I enjoyed helping to prepare the teas, the delicious sandwiches, egg, tuna or cheese, and cakes the players loved. Team members never failed to thank us for our hard work. It was a splendid time, lazing under the summer sun as a cricket wife. And cricket being a social game we would round off a good match with a trip to the pub to celebrate or to entertain our guests from another town.

Cricket was popular at the time, Fifth Street had three Caribbean teams, each with its own loyal band of followers. There was a Caribbean football team too and a netball squad. One night husband's club had a dance at the Town Hall and the support was phenomenal. A couple of hundred people all determined to have a good time. The promise of good food and music seemed to have lured everyone away from their television sets. It was a real Caribbean gathering with the kind of old-time atmosphere I wish we had caught on film to show youngsters how to enjoy themselves. Everyone all dressed up, drinks flowing, friends reunited. The ladies had done the catering for the event, I had prepared my special curry and my hard work had definitely paid off. The curry was a big hit and I'm not shy to say that quietly I felt well pleased with myself.

The organizers were even happier than I was. Not simply because the size of the crowd meant a good profit, but because a smoothly run function added to the club's high reputation. It was the kind of event where the night's melodies filled your head as it sinks sweetly onto the pillow. A truly wonderful occasion then with old-time Caribbean written all over it. Until, that is, someone asked me to dance late in the evening.

I can't remember who it was, it might have been one of my husband's mates, quite possibly it was someone who was close by and loved the number blasting from the sound system. We were on the way to get the car at the time, trying to ease our way through the thick crowd all hot and bubbly. A modest dance, the way a married woman dances with a friend and catches up with the progress of his family, that's all it was. But before the dance was over, he had stormed away from the function, drove off, and disappeared into the darkness. Was it because I was dancing with a friend? Imagine how I felt having to ask for a lift home from one of his friends. I was flabbergasted. I did not expect to be abandoned by my husband. What kind of husband would leave his wife like that? It was a question that would haunt me for years.

As a member of the band people would sometimes come up to me and say how much they had enjoyed a show. They appreciated what we were doing, they had requests for their favourite songs and, being West Indian, there were always a few people offering advice: such and such a song might enhance our repertoire, they might say, horns would add something to a particular song, we should play more reggae. That's West Indians for you. In my mind a man paying me a compliment was simply that: a thank you for a good night out, perhaps one of our songs had given him a helping hand in bringing round a woman who had been stalling him for months. He didn't see things like that, I soon learned. He would get jealous and sulky; I got the feeling he was saying, 'Hey, what about me?'

Not long after we got married, he began to press me for a child. We were still living in a single room, I pointed out, and the accommodation could barely take three much less four. But he did not see things my way and I did not see things his way and it became a duel between us. He took to hiding my contraceptive pills, when I scurried back to the doctor for a replacement batch he would turn the place upside down in a frantic hunt looking for them. Terrifying and scary to witness. It wasn't an ideal start to our life together. We're both young and healthy, I tried to reason with him, why the rush? But he refused to see my point of view and worn down by this constant battle I gave in. Not long after I fell pregnant.

As a young family with a baby on the way the council offered us a place. Then, as now, this was considered the posh part of town, the desirable, smart sector. We went to inspect the property and I fell in love with it immediately. A spacious semi-detached with a large garden and generous front lawn, this was the England of my dreams. My own home, my own garden! But there was plenty of work to be done. The house was brand new so we were free to add our personal touches. We painted and decorated it to suit our tastes, I bought curtains, and we installed new furniture. We were the first black family in the village and, when my son was born there in 1977, he had the honour of being the first black baby, if I could call it that.

When we moved in it didn't take the residents long to let us know what they thought of us. Times were so different in those early years, it's easy to forget how unpleasant prejudice could be. Some people gave us funny looks, others were more forthright. We were unwelcome, their cold stares and nasty looks made it plain we were intruders, why didn't we go back where we came from? They had a dozen derogatory names for us, we had to learn to ignore the nasty taunts or get dragged down their level. No doubt this was the common experience of Caribbean people throughout the country but we knew how to rise above those who taunted us or who sniggered as we went by.

And children weren't exempt; that, to me, has always been the sad part. Adults could shrug off the cowardly comments but the bewilderment of children was never easy to stomach. My daughter had more than a dose from her classmates in school; that hurt me more than anything the ignorant threw at me personally. I could see the puzzled, uncomprehending look on her little face, poor thing. Luckily, she was a bright child, and the respect this commanded eventually won over both children and teachers at her primary school.

Our new home was too far from Fifth Street to continue at the company so I gave up the job and found a new one closer to home. This was in a lighting and wiring company. To say that it required great skill would be an exaggeration. It involved placing the wiring in lightbulbs and the pay matched the degree of effort and knowledge required. But it was convenient. I dropped my daughter to school each day then took my son to the child-minder. After these, I made my way to work. When I got home, I did the hundred and one chores around the home.

My brother had emigrated to Wales and without his leadership; the band began to lose direction and eventually fizzled out. I was a full-time housewife now and, despite the odd hairy moment with my husband, it is fair to say, I was loving it.

In 1980 we bought the house. I can't remember the exact price we paid for it. The Conservative government had introduced legislation to enable council tenants to purchase their properties. Those who had occupied it for several years were rewarded with a hefty discount. The purchase was a good decision, it made financial sense. Both of us had steady jobs and, despite the usual marriage ups-and-downs and the occasional jealous outburst, we were getting on well. Many West Indians who had never thought of owning their property took advantage of the new scheme. We would have been fools not to jump at the opportunity.

We were settling into married life then, me and my husband. A child, our own home, husband's love of cricket, me getting used to life without my band, but little things began to get in the way. I suppose I had turned a blind eye to these quirks surrounding my husband, but, sooner or later, I would have to confront them.

One particular incident I can still recall to this day. The milkman had come to collect the milk money one Saturday and my daughter had gone to the door. It was a typical Saturday, the kind of day where you are glad for the rest after a long week at work. Having opened the door my daughter had then called for me to settle the bill.

In those days of corner shops, local post offices and small communities, the milkman was the cliché of a friendly face. Ever cheerful and humming as he placed your two white pints by the front door, whistling as he drove his battery-operated milk van in all weathers, he was the sign that things were right with the world. He knew everyone by name, he flirted innocently and outrageously. 'Is your mother at home?' he asked me that morning when I went to the door, in an unsubtle attempt at a compliment. 'You can't be the lady of the house, you're far too young!' As I chuckled at this, I heard my husband's voice, loud and grumpy and threatening: 'She's old enough!'

What could he mean? Why did he feel the need to express himself in this way? It didn't make sense. At the next house the milkman might compliment the wife on her lovely borders or some other intended double entendre, they would laugh and he would be on his way. Why did my husband have to read something into an innocent exchange?

We were pulling and dragging along now, me and my husband, the tension never far away. Something wasn't quite right but I couldn't figure what it was. My husband could be kind and considerate one minute, the next I would be on edge wondering which road he might take. He was uptight, anxious, restless, he was changing, and the course he was setting had 'disaster' written all over it. The man who had 'caught my eye' at that dance in Luton was becoming a different person, moody, sullen, unpredictable, I was constantly on my guard.

In January 1980, we had a christening party for my son. We hadn't had anyone around properly since we moved in and I was looking forward to showing off our home. Days, months of work had gone into getting it just the way we wanted it, the effort had transformed the shell of a building into a well-furnished home. After our private difficulties I suppose I saw the christening as a chance to rebuild our relationship. Perhaps my husband would come to realize how much we had achieved together. No one knew the full extent of our problems, of course, in a marriage it's not the kind of thing you broadcast. Marriages were about compromise, resolving conflicts, I reasoned, weren't they?

Friends came, and our families, there must have been over 40 people. It was a happy gathering, jolly, the drink flowed, the food was delicious. We had both put in a huge effort and the reaction of the guests was very pleasing. There was music and dancing, I was a proud mom for the second time and I wanted the world to know.

My son was a handsome child, cute enough for the women to genuinely coo over. My husband's friends were bowled over too. They were mostly his cricketing pals, the people he had spent years with both socially and on the field of play. Being typical West Indians, they loved to tease one another. If you were sensitive you wouldn't last long in their company. 'What a pretty baby,' one of his mates said to him in jest, I can't recall who it was. 'Are you sure you're the father?' A harmless throwaway remark, one to which a man would react with a mock backhander to his mate's right cheek or a quick witty riposte if he could think of one. Not my husband. What was meant to draw a laugh from those who were close by drove him into one of his silent rages. He stormed out of the house and into the cold night leaving me to entertain our guests.

A sense of astonishment descended on the proceedings. We stared at each other, not knowing what to say or do. His buddies who knew him well, who had seen flashes of temper, could only shake their heads in disbelief. Why would any right-minded person take offence at such a trivial remark? And even if he did, why disappear just like that? Why not simply say that he didn't appreciate such a comment, that his friend had crossed the line, and leave it at that?

My husband returned later that night when all the guests had gone, sliding into bed as though nothing had happened. I cried, for I didn't know what was going on, and he didn't seem to be himself, didn't even seem to know either. He had ruined the christening, had turned what was supposed to be a happy time into one that would tarnish us forever, yet it didn't seem to have occurred to him that there was anything weird in his behaviour.

I tried to console him when he returned in the early hours; I begged him to explain why he had abandoned the party and wandered off. But he had no explanation. He couldn't put into words what have driven him away, he had felt the need to go, that was all I could get out of him. I cried, cried a river, as the song says. I felt crushed, lost, helpless, embarrassed and ashamed for myself and for all those who had made the effort to support us. His reaction had been over the top and even more terrifying, he hadn't the faintest idea why he had done it. When I went downstairs the next morning the rain during the night had caused the drains to overflow and flood the place. I didn't know whether to laugh or cry.

Some months later he celebrated his birthday. He had a good relationship with his mother so she had posted him a card. It was a humorous card; the kind a mother would get for a loving son to chide him that he was getting old or to buy them both a cheap laugh. 'Twenty-five yesterday, twenty-six today, thirty by the end of the month: something like that.' It was just as well that she wasn't close by when my husband opened the envelope. Her innocent card had clearly offended him. I could see him tensing, growing more and more wound up as he read the innocent words. He snorted, clenched his fists, something had to be coming.

And sure enough there was. He wrote his mother a letter so ghastly that I was horrified at the contents. A boy who had been neglected or maltreated by his parents would have thought twice about putting on paper something so spiteful and vitriolic, and my husband had had an ordinary childhood as far as I could gather. That she was a mountain goat is the only accusation I could repeat here, I can't think of a single son who might have reacted with greater venom.

It was too much for his mother, as it would have been for any caring woman whose only intention had been to bring a smile to a son's face. She was soon on the phone crying, totally bewildered at his accusations and the bile of his words. How such an innocent card could have so sorely offended him, she wondered?]

What had there been in the card to offend him? I couldn't tell her, for what could I say?

The person that I had married was becoming someone I felt I didn't know. The quirks, the outbursts, the disappearances, I wasn't sure what was going on. In the beginning I had put my husband's behaviour down to the petty jealousies some men have. They want to be in control, these men; it is as though they feel a need to let a woman know that, and the world, for that matter. This behaviour was wearisome, annoying, but I had learned to deal with it. Now, though, it was clear that something more serious lurked within him. He was restless, uptight, constantly on edge. His behaviour was becoming increasingly erratic, he couldn't make sense of himself, and I was left feeling like a cyclist shunted to the side of the road on a dark wintry morning wondering what had hit me. Even with this feeling of unease I didn't fully appreciate what was to come.

Around midnight later that same year we were in bed on the point of sleeping when my husband suddenly shot up and began to scream. 'AHHHHHHHHHHHHHHHHHHHHHH!' As if in sympathy I shot up too, totally petrified. 'AHHHHHHHHHHHHHHHHHH!' he continued to bellow. It was so unexpected that I didn't know how to behave. I had never heard anyone holler like that. It was like the agony of a man being stabbed repeatedly with a knife, his screams pierced the night like someone being attacked with a hot poker. It was horrible, terrible, a dreadful and terrifying experience. He held his head, he screamed as though he was begging for mercy. A wounded animal, the rope tightening round its neck on the edge of a precipice, might make a sound like that. 'What's wrong?' I kept asking, 'please tell me, what the matter is?'

But I couldn't get a sensible answer out of him. Whether or not he heard me or knew of my presence there beside him I have no idea. The howling filled the room, the screaming, the terrible wailing. How long did it last? I don't know, it seemed like an eternity. I prayed for the children, I wondered whether the neighbours would call the police. My head throbbed, each piercing scream felt like it would snip off my ears like a barber's scissors. Eventually the screaming ended and I knew for sure then that my husband was ill. He was under the influence of some malign force, he was in desperate need of help. If he didn't receive medical attention he risked falling apart completely.

Still reeling from the events of the night, I walked my daughter to school the following morning and took my son to the childminder, trying to behave as normal as possible. Life didn't stop or go on hold, I told myself, there was no point in staying at home moping about or trying to figure out what had gone on and what to do about it. There was my steady work waiting to be done, plus a part-time job I had taken on to get some extra cash. It was difficult to prevent the night's episode playing away at the back of the mind but I reasoned that the sensible thing to do was to try to show the children that what they had heard was nothing to worry about. Things were under control, it was best to let them believe. If I got back into some kind of routine, I figured, the reasons for the incident might eventually became clear, and I might be able to help to sort out my husband's problem.

On the way back from the school to work, my mind told me to pop back home. A sudden thought, just like that. Just drop by the house and see how things are, a voice said to me, look in on the place. It was just as well I did. For whom did I see striding purposefully in my direction, coming from the house? My husband himself. Only, he couldn't have been himself. For my husband walked right past me as if I was a perfect stranger! Not with the haughty look of a man who, annoyed with wife, might pretend he hadn't seen her; not with the dirty look of someone you had offended who would throw you a glance then saunter merrily along. There was no sign of recognition on his part, he appeared to have crossed a shadow. His wife of six years seemed to be invisible to him!

My heart began to thump furiously. What had happened to the man I married not so long ago? What had triggered this new behaviour? That trance-like walk of his, where was it leading him, what had he done? I hurried home, my anxiety mounting, my head spinning, each stride adding to the sense of panic in me. Something had to be up, I could feel it. The terror of the previous night, now the quick retreat like a man who has just committed a robbery, there had to be some cause and worse, some horrendous effect. When I reached the house, I saw that the devastation was absolute.

A grey-black mess, a public destruction. There on the lawn the remnants of my clothes were sizzling, smouldering rags. Bottles of perfume popped away like firecrackers, the stench was dreadful. It was like a scene from your worst nightmare. My clothing, scattered and burnt, my creams and lotions and brushes, the dresses I had carefully chosen on so many shopping trips reduced to a heap, my home wear too. I scampered inside and had to cover my face in horror; some of the embers had been scattered on our bed. A demon possessed my husband, I now had no doubt. The talking to himself and answering back; the grunting and snorting as if there was a constant battle raging within him, he needed help, and urgently.

Even as I thought this, I remember seeing a slightly comical side to things. It must have been desperation, I suppose, an attempt to find some grain of comfort from the tragedy unfolding before me. When a situation becomes so dire that you have nowhere else to turn, humour is sometimes all that's left. So I sought the funny side in the devastation. A bonfire on the lawn just after breakfast, I thought to myself: what did the neighbours make of this? What were they whispering to each other over the phone or as they peered through the curtains, that black people were strange creatures with outlandish customs?

A quick temper, petty jealousies, the unpredictability of a man at odds with himself: that's how I had regarded my husband up till then. He could be funny, kind, gentle, sensitive, but he possessed an evil streak, or an evil streak possessed him, I didn't know which. But this was in a different league. Some trigger had been set off in him, a fuse lit, and the thought of what he might do began to scare me.

He was constantly arguing with himself and now he began to hurl demons out the bedroom window at night. Like two wrestlers in a ring they fought, before my eyes, one invisible, my husband bent on defeating the fighter who was plaguing him. Did he see himself that way? Was he truly aware of what he was doing? It got to the stage where I too began to question my eyes and my sanity.

The view of my husband I had held – quick tempered, a bit jealous and possessive - could no longer be true. I was convinced that some evil force possessed my husband, drove him down a road few of us would ever travel. That vicious streak had to be outside his control. To him, the demons he fought with were one hundred per cent real. The beings he tossed out the windows during the night were genuine as far as he was concerned; I have no doubts about that. No one would grunt and lift and hurl empty space out the window. In his mind I'm convinced he was ejecting a real person. But things were to get even worse.

More disappearances, more outlandish behaviour. My husband cleared out his car, tossed all the contents into the bin then walked away as though it was the most natural thing in the world. He then lobbed the keys into a lake and scarpered. His mother came on the phone crying during this period, my husband wasn't making sense, she said. He had obviously called her but what he was muttering was pure nonsense. Neither of us had the slightest clue about what was taking place in the tortured head of the man in our lives.

As he tumbled from one catastrophe to the next, it was only a matter of time before the law became involved. Thankfully the episode on the lawn had ended without anyone calling the police, his other unpredictable behaviours were domestic rather than public. But when one morning I received a call from a magistrate court in London, I wasn't totally surprised. It had been coming. The gradual escalation in the seriousness of his conduct meant that it was simply a matter of time.

My husband had been arrested for indecent exposure, the voice at the other end of the phone declared sternly, did I mind coming to see them? I closed my eyes and uttered a prayer, for the children, for myself, for my husband. I had never been to this part of London, it was an area I associated with drunks and lewd behaviour, the London of pickpockets and drug addicts. Nevertheless, in a state of shock, confusion and a slight trepidation, I caught the train and then the underground tube. I made my way to the court and found a man with a glazed emptiness in his eyes. He was blank, childlike, with no apparent appreciation of what he had done and the possible consequences.

A court hearing had been hastily arranged. Did I know the man who had been charged with indecent exposure, the official asked? Yes, he was my husband. Had I noticed anything odd in his behaviour? Had there been any signs that he might strip off his clothes in public? I listened to their account of what had taken place and answered truthfully. I revealed some of the things he had done, I heard the details of the shameful act. My husband was in urgent need of medical intervention, it didn't take us long to agree, medication and close supervision were essential if he was to come to terms with his condition. Take him home and make sure he got treatment, they advised, indecent exposure was bad enough, the next time could be more damaging for him.

So, somewhat to my surprise he was released into my care. He hadn't harmed anyone, the official pointed out when I protested that they had to share the responsibility for him, although his behaviour had been out of the ordinary, legally, there was nothing they could do. I could only sigh and pray that somehow, I would find the strength to carry on for I didn't know if and how I could cope. My husband was a sick man, removing your clothes in public wasn't the action of a human being in his right mind. The professionals had to help; it was their duty. My husband had shaved his head, I noticed, there was no hair on his body. His face was blank, this was a man with little inkling of what he had done and what was going on in the world about him.

We took the tube and caught the train back to the city. There wasn't much conversation between us, not proper conversation anyway. My husband was too far gone for that and I'm not sure what we could have said in any case. He was another man now, severely ill, incapable of day-to-day dealings. Whatever controlled him was in total charge, he was like a puppet under its direction. My husband wasn't a smoker yet there he was on the train that afternoon with a cigarette puffing away like someone who was fussy about the brand he inhaled. The voice that had commanded him to shed his clothes now had him on his knees in the train as it sped home through the West London countryside. I could only stare in disbelief as, on all fours, he tried to pick up from the floor every single flake of the cigarette ashes that had fallen there!

In this condition and without medical help it wasn't surprising that his actions would degenerate further. To begin with he didn't come home with me from the train station that day. I had no idea where he went, not now, not then. But later that night he came in with a bottle of whiskey. He poured some into a glass then placed a crucifix in it. I could only watch in horror as he offered my son the glass and suggest that he take a drink. His son, a mere child! My husband was gone, far gone. The crucifix now became an obsession with him. He drew pictures of crucifixes all over the house, he would perform magic with a crucifix on my busy Lizzie plant to make it grow even more.

One evening my son was on the toilet and I could hear my husband making a sound like a man working himself into a trance. It was a kind of mumbling,

rhythmic chant, but with a quiet menace to it - a mixture of grunting, groaning and panting, I didn't like the sound one bit. I went to the toilet and grabbed my son. With my husband in this mood no one was safe. When he saw me with his son he latched onto me and tried to throw me downstairs.

This was the final straw, I really couldn't take anymore. I phoned Mom and explained the situation. She came later that evening with our pastor. Religion would take over from medicine. They suggested exorcising him before he fatally damaged himself or someone else. Exorcise him, we agreed, drive out the tormentor.

You hear of neighbours recalling a murderer in their midst, saying what a nice, ordinary husband he was, how he cared for dog, how he mowed his lawn every Sunday, how much he loved his wife and family. The killing came as a complete shock, they agreed, they could not get their minds to marry the two portraits, the one a caring husband, the other a coldblooded murderer. And so it was with my husband. A sudden change now came over him now that we had visitors! The man who had earlier attempted to shove me from the landing underwent a total transformation. I couldn't believe my eyes or ears.

'Come in, Mom, come in Pastor,' he said with a wide sweep of the hand like someone inviting guests to tea, 'take a seat'. He knelt and prayed with the pastor, he accepted the healing hand placed on his head. I watched and listened, doubts beginning to grow in my own mind. My husband was the epitome of a God-fearing man that night, when they left I wondered if my mother and the reverend were whispering that I was the one who had gone insane. To my consternation, the moment they left, he turned to me and the mad look was back with him. 'Good,' he jeered, 'we're back to square one.'

I had informed my GP and the Health Visitor of the situation at home, I had reported how fragile and dangerous things had become. Having listened carefully they had referred my husband to the local hospital. But he came right back home. He had gone in voluntarily, I was told by the hospital staff, and as such, he was entitled to leave as and when he pleased. The authorities had no power to detain him, they could see that his conduct was out of the ordinary but, as professionals, they were powerless. And, even more heart-rending, throughout all this he was making out that I was the one who needed locking up, not him!

He took to wandering, and now he developed a new habit. He would go to any shop in town, eat and drink to his heart's content then get up and walk out as though it was the most natural thing in the world. In his mind no payment was necessary; every shop belonged to his father so he could do as he wished. I suppose the shopkeepers preferred not to make a scene or upset the other customers, one non-payment was better than driving the regulars away.

Up the steps he mounted, each one more outrageous than the last. One morning my husband sauntered to a neighbour's garage and wrote a cheque for a Mustang. Not an ordinary Ford or Volkswagen like the ordinary man working for a decent monthly wage, but a Mustang! Just like that! The proprietor phoned me directly, 'DD,' he said, 'we thought we'd let you know what your husband just did.' I didn't have to think about what to say to him. 'If I was you,' I replied, 'I would tear up that cheque.'

In my husband's mind we had money to burn and if we didn't that didn't matter. Nothing mattered in the world he inhabited; he did what came into his head, actions didn't breed consequences. He developed a habit of going to our bank and withdrawing our savings; what he did with the money I have no idea. We had joint accounts so the debts became my responsibility. I began to tear my hair out, our lives were spiralling out of control.

The episodes continued, each driving him deeper and deeper into his mental hole. He broke into cars; one of our neighbours accused him of trying to mess with her. The whole nightmare seemed as if it would never end. We slept in the same bed but I would be lying if I said we enjoyed a proper husband and wife relationship. This wasn't a man who saw himself as a husband with responsibilities, he acted on impulse, there was never a weighing up of right and wrong, the demons in him saw to that.

My husband hardly slept. You hear of people being possessed and that's probably the best description of his mental state at the time. No matter that he could appear normal to outsiders, he was mentally spent, severely so. He would get up in the middle of the night to fight with an imaginary foe. I would lie there hearing him arguing and cursing, I would watch as he tossed the opponents out the window, not knowing what to make of this unreal situation.

Or, unable to sleep, he might climb out of bed, go downstairs, and simply disappear into the dark night, even if it was freezing. Season didn't bother him, where he went I cannot say. But out he would venture, returning home later when presumably his mind had cooled or the demons were allowing him some respite.

On several occasions I managed to get him to see a GP. I would explain the situation as calmly as I could and my husband would sit beside me putting on such a normal front that I'm sure the doctor had doubts about the events I had related. That was probably one of the most unnerving things about him, the ability to switch to being a caring, listening husband and father in front of the professionals who needed to make an assessment of his state. People on the outside probably saw a man who was slightly eccentric, I'm sure that he managed to convince anyone who asked that I was making up the episodes I have described.

My husband had gone back to Guyana when his grandfather died, according to his mother. While he was there he had messed about with some woman, she had heard but she didn't have the details. The woman's family might have put obeah on him, his mother said, a particularly strong dose, and that was the cause of his 'disturbance'. I didn't believe in such things then and I still don't. Obeah exists only in the mind of those who want to believe such things. All I knew was that I was living with the destructive force that was him daily, and it was like being on daily hurricane alert.

My doctor advised me to leave the house when he eventually saw the strain I was under. I must have looked a wreck, I certainly felt like one. That was the best solution, the doctor suggested on one visit, get out, and hope that the situation improved. But, with two young children, where was I to go? Did he want my husband to beat me or kill one of us before the authorities did something that truly improved our lot? Did they wonder what it was like living with a man who was constantly having conversations and arguments with himself? He wouldn't take the medication they prescribed and they couldn't section him because he possessed the ability to appear relatively normal at times. In their minds they had done their bit. But, for me and the children, our lives were hell.

It got to the stage where I couldn't work, and my husband was too erratic to hold down a job. I was a physical wreck, the fitful nights and constant cleaning up in his wake had taken their toll. Our money ran out, I had to borrow from Mom to buy food for the family. But that was never going to be enough to solve our problems. As soon as I stocked up the voices in his head would command him to raid the fridge and empty the contents into the bin. To add to the disaster that was our life, he began to withdraw from our already negative accounts. When I alerted the bank in town, the crazy cunning in him sent him scurrying to the branch with his cheque book.

To escape the stress I left the house one day and went to Mom's place. A few hours away from the depression that was my home were all I sought. By this time Mom had moved. We chatted about this and that, it felt good to have a bit of time for myself and the children without having to wonder where the explosion would come from next. I wasn't there long before my husband arrived. I don't know how he knew where we were, he might well have followed us. My heart sank when I saw my husband. Was there no escaping him? Couldn't we have a moment's peace?

As I was thinking this he lunged at me. I was lucky. Lucky that my brother was there to restrain him, fortunate that others could see first-hand what me and the children had to put up with on a daily basis. His medication remained unopened; he was creating havoc wherever he went. But at least others could see for themselves the man he had become, one who couldn't be held responsible for his actions.

Like someone whose brain was scrambled after some catastrophic event he would go out and leave the front door open. There were none of the checks most people would routinely put in place. He often forgot the keys or misplaced them, and on his return he would simply smash the window and enter the house that way, without a second thought. With all that was going on I had trouble sleeping. I tried my best to protect the children from the turmoil but I could feel myself losing the battle. I asked the doctor for medication for my sky-high blood pressure and to help me sleep, but he refused. With young children in the house and my husband at large, he pointed out what should have been obvious to me: suppose you took sleeping tablets and fell into a deep sleep, he said, have you considered what might happen? I still shudder when I recall that morning in his surgery but things were to come to a head.

One day I was in the kitchen washing dishes when all of a sudden, I received this blow in the lower back. The force of the strike and the shock caused me to collapse in a heap on the floor. I was dazed and well and truly winded. It took me what seemed like an age to catch myself. What was going on? As I tried to struggle to my feet I found my husband standing over me with a crazed, twisted look of fury on his face. He was in the grip of a new fit of madness. The twisted, tortured look penetrated me as though he wanted to destroy me there and then, once and for all.

He had threatened me before but, apart from trying to throw me down the stairs with my son, he had never gotten physical. As I made to get up that day I could see a kitchen knife glinting in the half-light where I had stacked the wares and cutlery. I made to grab the knife. I had come to the end of my tether, had put up with his madness for too long. My husband was intent on our destruction, it was me or him. He might be ill, but illness didn't excuse the blow he had landed. Illness couldn't justify the constant pressure he applied to me and the children, no one deserved to live under such a threat. The knife flickered invitingly. It was him or me, the time had come to strike the decisive return blow.

But as I eyed the knife and was about to reach for it a voice from somewhere whispered to me, 'No. Don't. Think of the children: who'll look after them? With you locked away, what would become of them?' My mind cleared, the knife dulled. Blow for blow wouldn't help me or my husband, the problem called out for a more permanent solution, and a constructive one. 'What did you do that for?' I asked my husband, as he stood there staring at me, 'the blow could have maimed me.'

'You were having sex with the window cleaner,' he replied. He meant that I was actually having sex with the window cleaner at that moment, not washing up. What a state for a man to be in.

I took my son upstairs to sleep not long after, when things had calmed down. He was unsettled, a sixth sense must have told him that something serious was up. My husband followed me upstairs, grabbed the child by one arm, laid into him then dropped him. 'The two of you were having sex,' he said. He was out of control now, he was like a hound baying for blood. After I had managed to drive him away and settle my son I went downstairs for a rest. My head was throbbing, my back hurt, my body pained as though I had been in a boxing ring, I didn't know what I had done to deserve the life that was playing out before me. The ghastliest horror movie couldn't match the one I was living through. As I was lying on the settee, I heard him saying, as if in answer to someone berating him for a failure to carry out a task, 'Yes, she's still alive: I thought she would be dead by now. I will kill her tonight. I will do it tonight!'

At that point I called the GP. I could sense what was waiting round the corner, one of us was going to snap and this time there could be no doubt about the outcome. He had gone beyond threatening, and, if it came to that, there was no way I was going to curl up and accept a cold implement without giving as good as I got.

'You keep telling me you can't do a thing unless he harms us or kills us?' I said to the GP. 'You keep telling me to leave the house, where do you suggest I go?' He must have realized that we had reached the point of no return; the terror in my voice must have alerted him to the state my husband had driven me to. 'Pack a bag,' the doctor advised, 'get someone to take you to the bus station, and get on a coach to Oxford.' I obeyed. I hurriedly gathered what I could, packed them in a bin bag, grabbed the children and took off for a safe house in Oxford.

The house was a haven to a mix of people. I was met by a lady and shown our lodgings. Bleary-eyed, exhausted, I wondered if I looked as desperate as the group we were to lodge with. Women and girls of all ages shared this 'flea pit' of a house, most unable to shed a look of terror, fearful that at any moment the person they had escaped might somehow discover their whereabouts and their hell would begin afresh. I didn't have those worries. For the first time in months I felt secure; at last, after years of tossing and turning, I managed to get some proper sleep. Finally, the bleak, cold season of the life that began at one of our gigs was coming to its end.

The following day, I phoned Mom to put her in the picture. We were safe, I told her, there was no need to worry. The children were fine, a social worker was helping me to make arrangements for their education. I could hear the relief in Mom's voice for I knew how concerned she was for all our sakes. Next, I called work. The lighting company I've worked with had been good to me, allowing me time off when events at home took a turn for the worse; it seemed only fair to let them know my situation. I wasn't sure when I would be back, I warned them, I might not return at all.

For there was no way I could go back home and have my old life back. My husband was too unpredictable; I feared for our safety, there was no telling what he might do to himself.

During our first week in the safe house we were allocated a social worker. He visited us weekly. He checked that we felt secure, he explained his role and our entitlement under the law. He also arranged for some social security benefits to tide us over. I hadn't properly thought through what being in a safe house meant. We had fled there to escape my husband, but to me it was a temporary measure. I'm never truly comfortable unless I'm in my own place. The children needed their privacy to continue their education, I didn't want them to grow up carrying the stigma of months in a home for the desperate.

But the authorities wouldn't rehouse us, it wasn't their policy. They explained that the safe house was a temporary measure, it was best for us to return to Fifth Street. They were sympathetic to our plight, they said, but the onus was on me to get my life back on course. The children's schooling needed sorting, it didn't matter that we felt trapped, and didn't have the means or the solution to our problem. The education department began to apply pressure, my daughter had been out of school for too long, they pointed out, I had to make a decision about our future.

I couldn't go back to the house. Once my husband was there that simply wasn't an option. His behaviour was erratic, his mental state was deteriorating while we were there, who knows the point it had gone to with our departure. When I explained this to the authorities I was told to apply for legal aid. Get a separation, the legal people at the house advised, and apply for an injunction; that was the way forward. I couldn't see any other solution so I did as they suggested.

I went to Reading and did as I had been advised. My husband secured himself a lawyer and the separation process began. The lawyer was good, so good that I

was afraid that he might draw out the process or even win a victory for him. But he was fair. So when the judgement came he urged my husband to accept it. 'You're not helping yourself,' the judge advised my husband after hearing all the evidence, 'you're causing too much trouble for your family.' He was given seven days to get out of the house. I thought he might have challenged this and I had braced myself for a prolonged legal wrangle. But, to the relief of everyone, my husband accepted the judgement in its entirety.

After his departure we returned to our home. The safe house had provided a temporary solace but our own place was where we belonged.

Our return was very emotional. As the social worker's car cruised along the M40, winding its way through the flat, quiet countryside I was lost in contemplation. Life had galloped away from me during my marriage, what else did it have in store? Despite the disruption the children managed to remain optimistic, but how much had they been scarred? Gossip and rumours fed some of our people, they were never happier than when they could chew on your life like sweet tobacco. How much did they know about my troubles? I had been away from home for three months, what would be on the tip of the bitter tongues of those who were always in search of a prey?

My head was in a state. So much had happened in such a short time that it was a struggle to come to terms with what had gone on. Decisions about my life seemed to be in other hands, would I ever truly regain control?

I had travelled from the village of my birth to live with my distant aunt and with relatives I couldn't get close to, then had flown 3000 miles to be reunited with my mother and some of my siblings. Surprises both, coming out of the blue. Now I found myself journeying again to my home, admittedly, but this time with my own children looking across anxiously at me for guidance. But returning home brought new problems of its own.

Carrying the few possessions we had snatched in the haste to escape my husband's deteriorating mental state, we moved back to our home with the apprehension of an elderly patient after major surgery. My husband was out of our lives, I had phoned the neighbours and they confirmed that he had left. Now that the coast was clear I didn't want to waste a minute. I was eager to be in my own place again, to get the children back to school, to pick up our lives and begin a new chapter. After years of bombardment by a man with a 'split personality' I felt we deserved a break. But instead, it felt as though an enormous weight was attached to my back the instant I stepped over the threshold, a load that would take nearly five years of grit and hard graft to shift.

Months of unpaid bills were waiting for me in school, council tax, gas, electricity, insurance and, the gravest of them all, the mortgage. My husband would have gathered the letters and placed them on a chair or table to leave a clear path to the front door, but their importance would have been lost on a man who genuinely believed that all the shops in the world belonged to his father. Before I could think of fixing up the place, of new curtains and carpet and shades of paint or flowers for the porch, the pile of brown envelopes screamed out for attention. Open, open, they cried, dozens of them clamouring to be read before our lives spun even further into freefall.

The local council was threatening to take me to court for council tax I discovered, when I slit open the brown envelope atop the others. And, as if that wasn't enough, the building society demanded immediate payment. Letter after letter had remained unopened, they had assumed the worse - that we were reluctant to pay or were burying our heads in the sand, simply hoping that the problem would go away. With so many demands, the clear head I had managed to regain during the last three months quickly re-cluttered. As I read the threatening letters, I felt like I was being tugged by five people all at once, each wanting a part of me and none of them realising that I had nothing to give.

Envelope after envelope issued an ultimatum; it was a struggle to know where to begin. The companies weren't aware of the nature or extent of our problems and I doubt whether they would have cared. They provided a service; you had to pay for it, full stop. Large corporations had their overheads and directors rubbing their hands in anticipation of their bonus, they couldn't afford to get involved in the emotional lives of their clients. My name was simply that, an address and customer, an anonymous consumer of their products.

I couldn't face all the demands without professional help so with the assistance of the Citizens Advice Bureau I contacted a lawyer. She listened patiently to my woeful tale then wrote to all the companies outlining the position and asking for a sympathetic hearing. The responses were reassuring:

the small banking debts were written off, in time I managed to get the gas and electricity arrears sorted in manageable instalments.

We couldn't claim benefit at first and our mortgage went into arrears. With no money coming in, we were near rock bottom. Our most precious possession, our house, was now in jeopardy. We managed to get a lawyer on legal aid but by now the whole situation totally overwhelmed me. As each new demand came my head felt like it would explode. I couldn't think straight; I couldn't think at all.

Take the house, I suggested to the building society, we can't make the payments so why not get your money that way? The building society refused. If they took the house, they reasoned, they would have to find a home for us because there were young children involved. In the end the lawyer suggested that I come to an arrangement to show that I was willing to pay the mortgage. I offered 50 pence a week, that's how bad things had become. And to my utter surprise they jumped at it!

Now that I had come to an understanding with the building society about the mortgage, it was up to me to fulfil my part of the bargain. I set myself to work.

We had been given a sympathetic hearing, it could have been a dozen times worse I remember thinking when I had time alone to reflect later. From the moment I arrived in England I had pledged to stand on my own two feet, I wasn't going to alter that pledge now when the difficulties seemed almost insurmountable.

Not long after our return I received a call from my husband's mother. How much she knew about our trials and tribulations I wasn't sure but her words left me in no doubt about her feelings. 'When my son was well you wanted him,' she said bitterly, 'now that he is ill you don't.'

I remember my exact reply to her. I wasn't angry, but it was a struggle not to lash out verbally. 'If that's what you believe, you can believe it, you didn't come to see the havoc he was wreaking,' I told her, in a voice that left no doubt about how I felt.

So he had returned home. In a way I was glad that he was somewhere safe instead of wandering aimlessly. There were times when I feared the demons would overpower him and he would harm himself.

Within a week his mother called again. 'I want to apologize,' she said, and I could hear the pain in her voice and the weary sadness of a mother at the end of her tether. 'I hope you're not mad at me. My son tried to kill my husband; I now understand what you have been through.' I listened, for I knew there had to be more. She had called the police, she continued, she had had her son sectioned.

I felt sad, sorry for him, I still do. Despite what he put me through I don't believe he could have helped it.

At this point, trying to pick up our lives, I had no option but to take what was going to bring in some money. I would take my daughter to school, come back and do the same with my son then rush to my job at the lighting factory. After work I would pick up the children, go shopping for a lady then hurry to an evening cleaning job; anything to clear some of the debts.

My husband was far away in a high security unit where he could be properly cared for; it would be up to us to get our lives back on track. I used to visit him with the children and our social worker. His was a genuine illness; I couldn't simply cut him loose. It was painful to see how he had degenerated. I felt sorry for the man who had given me his name. But he was mentally ill and the hospital was the right place for him if he stood any chance of recuperation. The staff could ensure that he took his medication so there was an outside chance of him getting better.

On one visit one of the patients in the unit seized my son and wouldn't let go. Pleading with him didn't help, he seemed to have supernatural strength. It took three members of the staff to prise my husband from his grasp. Visiting was too risky, we decided after that incident, so we didn't go back to see my husband.

One of the doctors who were treating him asked me, 'Do you think somebody did something to him?' Coming from a medical man the question surprised me. I told him I didn't believe in superstition. 'Don't rule it out,' he responded, again to my surprise, 'I worked in the tropics, there might be something in it.'

My husband secured an accommodation that the state secured for him. He was incapable of working because he still suffers from the same complaint, the delusions haven't left him. If he goes for a job, he wants the manager's role, in the same way that he used to eat in a shop and leave without paying because, in his mind, the shop belongs to his father. He spends his days wandering from one place to the next, I've been told.

I went to visit him and his Mom with my son in 2013. When we got there his mother said, 'Be careful'. My husband looked old and haggard. He recognized me and believes that we are still married. 'Why aren't you wearing your wedding ring?' he asked. What could I say?

His mother died in December 2014. My son and I went to the funeral. My husband looked rough; he was like a man in his 70s, his toothless face hairy and sunken.

CHAPTER EIGHT

Post – Marriage

THE JOB AT THE LIGHTING company had been kept open for me, I returned to it determined to show them how much I appreciated their generous gesture. The pay wasn't fantastic but I needed the money. And, despite the low rate, I wanted to thank them for their patience and understanding during the horrendous times of which they had but a vague notion. With the burden of my husband's unpredictability removed from my shoulders, I set out to work like a Trojan, I had to. I hated the idea of being in debt. I had been to a place where the reins of my life had been snatched from my hands, I had no intention of being dragged down there again.

By this time, I was on good terms with the neighbours. Time had moved on, West Indians were no longer 'novel and trouble'. Our presence was more or less accepted, only the ignorant spouted their bigoted insular nonsense. But how much my neighbours knew of my situation I'm not sure. They didn't ask and it wasn't the kind of thing to blabber about. If they had suspicions about what had gone on they didn't mention it; they greeted us warmly now and accepted us as a part of their small community. We were on such good terms that they brought my daughter home after school, allowing me time to cook and get myself ready for my other jobs.

Looking back now, I'm amazed at the energy I managed to find during these testing times. Where it came from I had no idea. I seemed to be constantly on the move, doing this, doing that, seeking out opportunities to add a little income to that of my steady job. People sometimes say to me, 'DD, you had it easy, didn't you? Gold records, tours to so many exotic countries: I wish I had your life.' If they had come across me during that manic phase, dashing from pillar to post, desperate for what I could find to raise 10 pounds, they would have known better. I did so many jobs, I cleaned so many toilets I'm amazed that I found time to sleep. I washed, cleaned and shopped for an old lady locally, fixed her tea, then rushed to an evening cleaning job. Tiredness couldn't stop me: I needed money, the bills were going to be paid by hook or crook.

At the time Income Support was available for people in my situation, a single wage, quite low, made up with part-time work. I made some inquiries and was invited for an interview by the support team. If I stayed at home and claimed this 'benefit', I was informed at the short interview, I would only be £12 a week worse off from my current situation of three jobs.

All that racing around from place to place, the long days and tired aching legs, was it truly worth it, I asked myself after I had listened to their explanation of how the benefit system operated. Was it truly? Some people might have been tempted into collecting this government 'support' for simply 'expressing a desire to work', but not me. I preferred to work for my bread; the idea of staying up late at night watching television and moping about during the day trying to fill time could never attract me. Besides, the extra £12 I collected from my labour could be put to good use in the home, or catching up on the arrears.

But the early months after our return from the safe house were hell, albeit in a different way. Every penny was precious, each bill paid a weight off my shoulders. I didn't burden my friends with my problems, they saw me smiling and happy but they had no idea of the depth of the hole I had tumbled into. Trips to the pictures with the children were few and far between, there were no holidays, and certainly no expensive toys.

The children had to make their own entertainment as little by little, I began to reduce the debt. And why not? I consoled myself when I felt a little guilty that they were missing out on what their friends took for granted. Why moan about what others possessed, didn't we get by without them? Isn't that what we did in the Caribbean when I was young? Thankfully, neither my children showed any signs of being blighted by the experience. Their resilience warmed my heart. As long as I was happy then so were they, it seemed: I got the impression that they would have eaten bread and butter for weeks on end if that was all we could afford.

My only indulgence during this oppressive stage of my life was a weekly keep-fit class at the Methodist Church. I was determined to keep my figure no matter what it took. In cold weather or warm, my poor boy would have to sit on a wooden bench watching a bunch of mad women bouncing and stretching and grimacing for an hour to the strains of some disco song. He kept his thoughts to himself: I wonder what he told his little friends.

Domestically, the pressure eased with each passing month, the proverbial light appeared at the end of the tunnel.

It took me four years to clear all our debts. With the help of the neighbours who offered to look after the children while I worked, after scurrying from job to job to get whatever was going, all that remained was the mortgage. It had been like walking with my eyes firmly fixed on the road beneath my feet, but now that journey was ended and I could lift my head to face what was before me.

After a successful set of GCSEs my daughter had won a place in the sixth form at the high school and my son had transferred to middle School. They were both good students, able to concentrate on their studies despite the traumatic experiences we had been through. Being older, my daughter obviously had some understanding of her father's condition, but my son didn't show any of the signs. He didn't ask about his father, his friends and school appeared far more important.

And he loved his friends as much as they loved him. They would come knocking for him after school to go to the playground, I swear he was out of the house more often than in. At the age of three he could write his name firmly and confidently, before he was five he covered the walls of the house with the names of his closest mates and family members. His friends flocked to our home to see their names, they gasped in wonder at his ability to spell and write so well. For his third birthday he wasn't interested in toys like his school chums, he wanted a calculator!

The Caribbean community had grown during the time when, whatever angle I considered it, I was like a mere spectator to my own life. First my husband plunging us into the kind of state you wouldn't wish on an enemy, then having to dig ourselves out of the financial hole in which we had found ourselves. It had been like a grim perpetual winter. Wrapped up against the elements, fighting the frostbite and chill of the wind, it felt like racing home only to find that the central heating had broken down. But I had succeeded in shaking off the icy cloak of winter, I could re-join the world, and try to make up for what I had missed.

The community had grown, it had also changed. Immigration from the Caribbean had virtually ceased, it was now a question of second or even third generations in the town. Few of our children could speak or understand the West Indian language; the Caribbean was becoming a place where they went for holiday, not countries to which they felt some psychological attachment. Some young parents couldn't cook Caribbean dishes, for others it was simpler and quicker to bring up the children on takeaways or fish and chips. After years of hard work, the first arrivals were retiring, some to look after grandchildren, others back to the sunshine. And all this had been going on without me really noticing!

But some things hadn't changed. I remember the summers of the mid-eighties with a special fondness because they were the last years of grand Caribbean weddings at the Town Hall. My nephew, got hitched, and several of his friends, male as well as female. Five hundred, maybe six, enjoying the atmosphere of a West Indian marriage, is there a more wonderful sight? Children listening to our music and learning our dances, sampling our cuisine and expressing themselves as only they can: what a welcome relief for someone who had almost forgotten what good times were like.

I was happy again now. Not ecstatic, just plain and simply relieved. I had spent years just trying to get by, now I could begin to look forward, to make plans, to consider other jobs, to think of learning to drive. Like a tornado out of the blue skies my husband had sent everything crashing, but now he was over, and the sweet calm of normality descended on us.

But not quite. Occasionally my husband somehow managed to escape the 'secure unit' and would find himself at the house, but he was never any trouble. I mustn't paint him as evil or conniving. Friends from the local pub might accompany him when he came by, he still lived his own version of reality. This was his home, what was more natural than to invite a few friends round? I wonder if the mates he brought to the house to continue their drinking session suspected, or knew about his true condition. In his mind we were still married, still together as a family. When the police came to escort him back to the unit he always went without a hint of trouble.

CHAPTER NINE

Recording

OUR HOUSE WAS SITUATED IN a close. The location gave a good view of the traffic and passers-by. One lunchtime I looked out from my cooking and saw a man approaching the house with a guitar. As he came closer I recognized the bespectacled figure, he was a respected local musician, also originally from SVG. Whatever he had to say I knew I wouldn't be interested. Music had gone out of my life in more ways than one. I have had a glorious spell singing in the band, but with my brother's departure to settle with his family in Wales, all the band members had moved on in their separate destinations.

This respected musician rang the bell that midday but I wouldn't answer. A quiet life was what I craved, a life without hassle. I knew that my daughter had seen him and had heard the bell, and I thought of telling her to open the door, smile sweetly and inform him that I wasn't in. 'Mom said to tell you she isn't in.' In my mind I could just imagine her saying that to him and her hand racing to cover her mouth when she realized what she had done. So instead of putting her in a situation she might be uncomfortable with, I trudged wearily to open the door. This guy is a small thin man with an affable manner and infinite patience, he didn't seem put out by the wait. I invited him in and we sat and made small talk for a while, not realizing the impact this would have on my future.

It didn't take him long to turn the conversation to the business he had come to discuss. He had seen me with my band; he liked my singing very much, he said, what was I up to these days? I thanked him and waited for the next line, for I knew that he wouldn't have come all this way to dole out gentle compliments.

There had to be some proposal, an invitation of some kind to put to me. 'I've written some songs, DD,' he came quickly to the point, 'I wonder if you could record them for me.'

He had a studio and producer lined up, he continued, as I took in this suggestion and played with it in my mind. My agreement would set the ball rolling. Where was I to begin my answer to this man who had taken the trouble to come to my home? Was he aware of the strait-jacket from which I had just recently managed to extricate myself?

Outside the family I didn't discuss this painful aspect of my life. When people asked, I said as little as possible: it was too easy to try to explain only to end up as a villain. So I decided not to say anything about what had gone on to him either. The children were young, I took a roundabout route instead, giving away as little as possible, and hoping that he would understand. Their schooling was at a very delicate stage, I continued, I couldn't let them slack for a moment and ruin their prospects of university. I was responsible for them, time in the studio would mean time away from helping them with their studies and that wouldn't be fair, would it?

I suppose a part of me was mildly excited at the thought of recording, but another suggested caution. Performers and recording artists are two separate species, I sussed even then, some can move effortlessly between both styles but, if they are honest, the majority of singers would admit that they prefer one to the other. In a live band a performer feeds off the audience, you can create and improvise according to its mood and the general atmosphere. A band can respond instantly to a hot crowd by repeating a verse or a chorus, or you can build slowly over the course of a set and reach for a crescendo.

When my band truly clicked, we surged onstage all guns blaring and kept that peak throughout the night.

A studio held out as many prospects as challenges, I thought to myself as we sat there, the respected musician keen to have me give life to his words. What would it be like singing with no audience to please? Who would I be singing to or singing for? How would I gel with musicians who were unfamiliar to me in surroundings that might take months to get accustomed to? 'No,' I told him that afternoon, after putting these questions to myself and answering them as candidly as I could. 'Thanks for thinking of me, but I'm not sure that I could record an album of your songs, too many other things going on in my life.'

But he was persistent. The smile came out, warm and sincere, the voice kept its gentle persuasiveness. He must have noticed me weighing up the pros and cons in my mind, maybe he truly believed that I would be the person to do justice to his material, whatever the reason he wouldn't take no for an answer. 'Think about it,' he suggested in his soft Caribbean voice with its subtle lilt, 'I'll be back in a fortnight.' He put a cassette of his music in my hand, and I placed it to one side the moment I closed the door behind him.

When he had gone, I put the visit to the back of my mind. I was enjoying the evenness of my life, the job, the children, getting the house into the shape I wanted. A million and one little jobs needed doing. I didn't want to think or even dream along the lines of becoming a singer. I had had brilliant times with my band, it was better to be remembered that way than to become a recording artist no one could spare the time to listen. The next time I saw Mom, I told her about the offer and the decision I had given him. Where I had hesitated, part of me feeling secretly honoured that he had chosen me, another fearing the unknown, Mom was decisive. 'What have you got to lose,' she put it to me after I had reeled off chapter and verse, 'why not give it a go?'

Her response surprised me both in its content and swiftness. I don't know what I was expecting, but had she said it was too risky I would have accepted her advice. Had Mom pointed out the need to stay close to the children that too would have made sense. Instead, she wanted me to give it a try! As promised, he duly returned for the reply with the same calm manner, gently coaxing, never hectoring. 'I've changed my mind,' I gave him the news he was clearly hoping for. 'I'll do the album.' I could see the thin face brighten and the beam of happiness that soon the face couldn't hold back. 'But on one condition,' I added. 'This will be the first and the last.'

He was happy, extremely so, he couldn't hide his delight. All the months and years he had spent composing the songs, the cold winter nights and luscious summer evenings, and now they were about to come to life! In this same quietly excited state he drove me sometime after, and introduced me to the producer and record company owner. They had obviously had discussions before and both seemed completely at ease. The producer was a tall Jamaican with what to me was a weird dress sense, and, at the time, two or three other hopefuls were signed to his record label. We would have what I would call an uneven relationship, but, at that first meeting, relationships were the last thing on my mind.

'Sing something,' the producer said, in the weary tone of a man who has heard dozens of people who can sing a single verse and chorus only to falter by the second. I can't remember the song I chose or how many verses I offered up, but his response was immediate; 'Wow,' he grinned, nodding to indicate that he had heard something out of the ordinary, 'fantastic, amazing!' I was pleased that he liked my voice: as a singer you are either hot or cold: either the voice delivers or you disappoint yourself and the listener. Put on the spot I had delivered to a man who had vast experience as a producer, and that gave me a warm feeling inside. He was confident that I had the ability to do justice to a song, I would be an asset to his 'stable'. And so, without meaningful discussions or contracts or explanations, it was down to recording the album and whatever else the producer had in store.

I had never been in a studio before. The studio was an average affair. And even now, after years of recording and performing, I'm still amazed that such a sterile environment could burst into life and result in music that can reduce you to tears or send you dancing up the stairs and down. Claustrophobic, sealed off from the world without a thought of comfort for musicians or singers, that first floor studio was the ultimate in functionality but it was to have a great influence on my future.

The recording studio had shocked me and made me anxious in equal measure at first. How would I fare in this bubble? In the band I had the others right alongside for support, a nod and smile to tell me when my singing was truly on form, an encouraging signal to get me back on track if I slipped into automatic mode. My first time in the studio sent my anxiety levels off the scale. It felt like asking a girl accustomed to practicing to shoot for goal in her school playground to play a netball game in front of an audience of 10 thousand.

Perhaps I felt slightly intimidated by the paraphernalia of recording: the long mixing console with hundreds of twinkling dials. Again, it might have been the natural apprehension we all have as we tiptoe into the unknown. It's not easy to prevent the stomach churning and wishing you were back in the heart of your family, when confronted with the unfamiliar. But I had given my word and I didn't intend to retract it. Not from the composer, not from the producer who now said little after his initial flattery. Yet, on entering the room and slipping on the 'cans' I could feel a slight panic within me. A voice somewhere deep within me said, 'DD, what are you doing here'?

The sensation of the headphones clinging to my ears that first time was distinctly eerie. Was it the amplified sound of my breathing that I feared would be captured on the recording? Or was it the beating of my heart that came across as loud as the frantic thumping of a bass drum? It would take me a while to get accustomed to the unnaturalness of performing in a studio. Weeks would go by before I learned to relax, to let my musical instincts take over. I had sung in public for years, I had to remind myself when little doubts nagged away at me, why worry about having my voice recorded?

Performing live, you have the band with you. You sing and dance, satisfy the audience and everyone goes home happy. No two shows are the same, even if you sing the identical songs in the identical order with similar audiences: that is the essence of Caribbean music: surprise, unpredictably, the senses heightened by not knowing precisely what is going to strike. I had never heard my voice, what I sounded like I could only imagine. And now, for the first time, for good or ill, I was about to have my singing captured.

And it was a shock. We can recognize our friends by their voices and unless family members deliberately put on a heavy accent we can identify them from a sentence, if not a single word. But what we sound like is a mystery. The pleasant sound we take for granted comes over as hollow and stilted when we play back a tape recording of it. To hear myself singing was like listening to a stranger. It took weeks before I got accustomed to standing to record a song and hear the playback and say, 'My goodness, that's me.'

Impatient and business-like, the producer was pleased when I finally got the hang of things. Music was a commercial enterprise; I could tell that this was uppermost in his mind from the way he sighed and snorted. He was in the business of making money, I would later discover, singers and musicians were commodities, pleasing the public was all that mattered. But, as the sessions progressed I could feel that this philosophy was going to try us all.

The record company was small, with three or four singers on its books. It used a single musician, supremely talented, who could play most of the instruments we needed for a production. But I was so frustrated with him at times because to me, he played by his own rules. Like a groom keeping the bride waiting at the altar for hours, he would swan in late, without even the excuse of severe traffic, armed only with his disarming smile and the knowledge of his outrageous musical ability would win everyone over.

The producer would book the studio for 2p.m. and we would wait patiently only for the producer to turn up at three or even four. No excuses, no apology. Studio time was expensive, he must have known, but that didn't seem to bother him. He was extremely gifted, in constant demand, and I wondered if he felt that his accomplishments gave him a license to do as he pleased. 'Where is he?' the producer would pace up and down angry and growing angrier, snorting and cursing and muttering and worse, 'where the hell is he?'

It is strange to think that so much depended on one man, but it did. He was the ultimate artist, an incredible arranger who would be my producer down the line. Any song you brought to him he would pick up after a couple of bars; to hear him perform was to wonder at his gifts. He played guitar, he programmed the drums, he was a wizard on keyboards. Just as well he fell down on horns or we might never have finished the album. But, to give him his due, apart from his Caribbean disregard for time, the moment he arrived he got down to business and another session would go with a bang.

Recording was very demanding. Each session took a lot out of me, physically as well as mentally. When this respected musician couldn't drive me to London, I would take the train and make my way from there. Every Sunday for what seemed an eternity I was in London giving my all and praying to get the album over and done with. In cold autumn or rainy summer, I got on that train and rehearsed the songs we would be recording later. I practiced at home, humming the lines to myself even as I worked.

Not that the producer appeared to appreciate the sacrifices I was making or the domestic situation I was coming from. As the months went by I had expected a professional working relationship to develop between us, one in which he could map out what he was expecting musically and share his plans for say, the upcoming sessions. I thought we would get beyond sharing a quick takeaway during recording, that he would ask about my children, or at least get to know their names.

That didn't happen. What did he care that I was on a train home after midnight on a cold winter night wondering how my children were? I came, I sang, I left, another song ticked off: feelings didn't come into it.

I was so fortunate to have a mother with such a good heart and the willingness to allow a daughter the freedom to follow a dream. She looked after my children for me, she put up with my late nights and grumpy moods without a word of complaint.

For someone with a history of getting the best from his signings I found the producer harsh and unsympathetic. He probably didn't see me as a long-term investment. When he looked at me, the image he had was probably one of crispy pound notes to line his pockets until the next singer came along. After my brief 'audition' where he had expressed his appreciation of my talents, he seemed to have grown cold. I don't know what he was expecting of me. Perhaps he regarded me as a small-islander new to the industry so he could treat me in the dismissive manner too many people in music seem to thrive on. 'SHE FLAT!' he would grumble when I wasn't at my best, 'FLAT, FLAT, FLAT!'

'She is the cat's mother,' West Indians will tell you, no woman wants to be called 'She'. It is the ultimate insult on the same level as cursing someone's mother. He must have known that it would hurt me for he said it loudly and often and clearly for my benefit. Not for him the understanding approach, an arm round the shoulder, the soothing words we all need now and then: 'don't worry, you're doing fine: but just shift it up a gear next week.' Not for him these endearments. If looks could injure he would have had me swathed in bandages in that hell of a studio on too many days to count.

But, if I'm honest, some of it had to be my fault. I didn't assert myself, I almost let him trample over me. I had gone into something

I didn't know much about without asking questions, taking people far more experienced in that field at face value. Believing that those I was working with had my best interests at heart, I was too meek, too ready to oblige, when I should have been saying, 'Hang on, wait'. I was working at my other job and raising a family on my own, then making my way to London, sometimes so tired that it was an effort to go, and having to return home late, I should have told him to his face all the things I kept bottled up.

But he spent his money on booking the studio, paying musicians and engineers, he had the connections I would need when the album came out: that's the way I think he saw it. I meekly accepted what I was told, I tried to interpret the songs in the way producer, composer and arranger suggested. I would be guided by their superior knowledge of the industry and their desire to place another singer on the road to success.

It took one of the other female singers on the label to show me the way to treat the label owner and, in retrospect, I probably should have taken a similar stance. He had made some derogatory comment about her singing and she laid into him with venom and truly let him have it. Another comment from him and I'm convinced she would have decked him there and then. I don't think he attempted to undermine her after that incident. But that wasn't my style: I hadn't been brought up to swear and rant and throw my arms about like someone who has truly lost it: I tried always to keep some measure of dignity. I would try to explain my position calmly; I didn't go in for the rough stuff. But from that day the vicious nature of the industry came into focus for me, it taught me that in order to survive you have to give as good as you get.

By this time, I was getting fed up. Fed up, frustrated, angry, tired, call it what you will. I just wanted to get the album finished so I could get back to the other half of my life. Recording was nibbling away at my existence. There were too many late nights in a cold railway carriage. Rolling home in a car at 3:a.m. and trying to snatch a few hours' sleep before work at eight were testing me to the limit.

But I never let my standards slip. I was never totally satisfied with a recording, I was always looking for ways to improve. On the journey home I would review the session, sometimes happy with my delivery, at other times trying to think of how I might build on my performance. A word, a phrase might come to mind, a line of the chorus I could give a slightly different emphasis. That's the lot of a singer, we are seldom satisfied. There is always that nagging feeling that we haven't quite done justice to a composition. It is the professionalism in us, I suppose, we want every performance to be perfect; the slightest deviation from this and we are unhappy with ourselves, with the thought that we haven't done our talent justice.

So the recording sessions began to take their toll on me. No singer exists in a cocoon and I was a prime example of a woman with the dizzy sensation of winter snapping through her clothes to the bones. I couldn't shake off the stresses of work and family life; I took them to the studio in one form or another. Physically, mentally, the act of voicing a track is quite demanding, the producer at the time grew more and more irritable and my enthusiasm began to wane. 'She flat,' he hurled the insults in my direction, 'flat, flat!'

To me, this attitude was extremely disrespectful. Getting a record out was joint enterprise, there had to be mutual trust to derive the best results. I was trying my best under difficult circumstances, I could do without the scorn heaped on my shoulders. If he had felt that I lacked the qualities he wanted from his performers, as an experienced producer he would have said so at the audition that first day.

But he hadn't. He had praised my performance then, he had added that I had a natural talent. He had released a single before the album was finished. The recording had given me goose pimples then and is still popular today. Even he couldn't hide his pleasure at my rendition of the track he had composed. The Jamaica Tourist Board would later use the song in their promotions; he ought to have been a bit more sensitive to someone who had so impressed his countrymen that they used her song to attract tourists from across the globe. That the song had topped the reggae chart should have made him stop and think, 'Hey, I need to cherish this lady: if she can deliver such a massive hit in the reggae chart, what else might she have up her sleeve?'

But I don't think he saw things like that. So, despite having a massive hit in the reggae charts, completing the album became one long frustrating struggle for all concerned. Our second single was the stumbling block. Try as I did I couldn't get it right. One of his composition, it seemed simple enough, but every voicing met with derision. 'Put more feeling into it,' the producer would growl, 'it's coming out too flat.' When, like a girl struggling with her homework I asked what my performance, lacked he couldn't tell me. He knew how to criticize but he couldn't offer a single constructive suggestion. His annoyance grew and mine quickly caught up, especially with myself.

The slow tempo of the song called for precision. Each phrase, every word asked to be delivered with longing but not sentimentality. All the versions I had laid down had been reasonable, I felt, some I would even have rated as good. But his requirements were for something more, some quality he felt was missing but probably couldn't put into words. To my extreme disgust, he even threatened to offer the tune to the other female singer on the label.

All these were on my mind one Sunday on the way to the studio. To be honest I didn't know how much longer I could continue. Too many thoughts were going round in my head, I couldn't see the point in carrying on, paying a fortune in train fares, living on takeaways when recording, living this lonely and miserable existence.

There were no discussions about if, when and how much I would be paid, I objected to being called, 'She' instead of by my name. The first song was doing well with Caribbean listeners, but I had no idea of the exact sales or how the marketing was progressing, for he didn't share those details. With so much going on I felt miserable and full of self-pity. Perhaps it was time to quit, I had tried my best, maybe it was time to move on to something new, to get back to life with my children.

When I got to the studio, all these thoughts and exasperations were swirling round in my mind. I couldn't shift them as I placed the cans to my ears as I had done dozens of times before. The cold grimness of the room simply added to the melancholy I had dragged in with me from the journey. Like the smell of cooking that lodges in the fabric of your clothes the bad feelings lingered, frustration gnawed away at my insides. All those long journeys on a cold smoky train or on the motorway, the oily takeaways instead of proper food, the studio that had sounded glamorous when my composer first described it and in which I was expected to perform at the drop of a hat: was this what my life been reduced to?

I did one take that day. A single voicing. Standing perfectly still I closed my eyes and tried to interpret the words he had written, perhaps on a cold winter's night when he was lonely, the way he would have wished. I blocked out the outside world, I wasn't conscious of anything but the music coursing through the headphones asking to be sewn to the words. With my eyes firmly shut, I allowed my whole being to be at the mercy of the shifts of the rhythm track. I went cold after my efforts. It had been a struggle, but now it was over.

As I emerged from my trance-like state I could see the producer's eyes light up. 'Wow.' There was an unmistakable smile in his normally cynical eyes. The song that would sell millions and have over 1.1 million hits on you tube was born on that Sunday spring day.

The song has a simple message. A woman is torn between two lovers, you can imagine her at a dance with her husband but with her lover pining for her in a distant corner of the hall. She loves them both, would steal away quietly to spend a few brief moments with her new love if she could, but, respecting the consequences, wishes that she could be 'in two places at the same time' so that she can share her love. It's the classic lover's dilemma, the comforting staleness of the familiar versus the temptation and danger of the new. And finally, after numerous versions, I had succeeded in rendering his words the way he had hoped for.

I left the studio feeling drained but serene. The final session, no more loud sighs and dirty looks. My whole being was filled with the serenity of a long hot Caribbean Sunday, with families strolling to church in the morning, the children powdered and full of expectation, their parents dressed in their best, praying for guidance and good fortune. In the afternoon, after lunch and a siesta the family might saunter to the beach for a dip in the sea, poor but secure, alive to the beauty around them, the flowers, the landscape, the comforting warmth of the high sun. Finally, I felt at peace with myself.

There was lightness to my steps on my way to the car park to prepare for home. My obligations were over, I had fulfilled my part of the bargain. I had made a promise to my composer and delivered, the album had taken from August to April, a lot longer than we had anticipated, but now it was over I could sense the relief all round. The mixing and other minor arrangements remained, but my job was complete. The arranger, engineer and producer would take over now, refining, mixing, getting the songs in just the right shape to unleash on the public. What the album and the individual songs did upon release would be up to the listeners of Britain.

CHAPTER TEN

Crossover

THREE OR FOUR SONGS FROM the album stood out as potential singles. After adding background vocals and listening to the final product, I must say I was impressed. Months of hard slog had resulted in a piece of work of which I was justly proud. It was a question now of releasing one song, gauging the response, and marketing it successfully. Air play was crucial, and this meant having the right contacts or making some. I was to discover that this wasn't as easy it sounded.

This was the era of an independent reggae circuit with a reggae chart featuring mainly Jamaican imports, and some home-grown Caribbean music. A couple of thousand records might get you into the reggae charts, a record sold rapidly then disappeared as swiftly as a minor comet in the icy emptiness of deep space. Even where sales were in tens of thousands the national charts were out of reach. The outlets that contributed to the prestigious BBC charts made a point of excluding music from the Caribbean, although they strenuously denied it.

We screamed and thumped our fists in frustration at this blatant injustice but they disregarded us then as they do now to a large extent. So we were left to do our own thing. In the main West Indian buyers wanted music to dance to, each dance sprang another and so forth, until a new craze hit the town. As the dance shifted so did the music, until it was impossible to tell which led the other, the dance or the song.

Being small-scale and catering mainly for the Caribbean public, independent producers were happy to sell the quantity of records they had bought from their suppliers at a modest profit until the next batch of records came along featuring the latest 'sensation'. Male or female, the new 'star' thrilled for a month before someone else latched onto their idea and pushed their song into a higher orbit. As outstanding as some of these songs were, singers or producers seldom went into wider promotion for they knew what they were up against. The barriers against West Indian artists were immense; artists broke through onto the national charts as novelty value or where the sales were too prolific to ignore.

This was the situation that my producer faced on completion of the album. He knew that he had a couple of potential hits on his hands but he had to contend with an industry that gave the impression that it was only interested in Caribbean artists with dreadlocks who smoked prodigious amounts of herb, or who were scandalous, especially in an exotic or sexy kind of way. His contacts were people of the same stature, hustlers, some have called them, cut from the same cloth, without access to the 'big boys'.

The BBC and English radio stations looked down on these independent producers with the superciliousness of a lord detecting a crumb lodged in his rich moustache. They were small fry, upstarts, people they could easily ignore. A hundred English music producers, it was rumoured, each with a potential star on board, were prepared to sacrifice their dignity and more to buy air play, so why on earth should the people in high places give air time to songs with what they considered, 'minority appeal'?

My producer didn't have the knack of forging contacts and his brusque manner obviously didn't help. He was quick to brand anyone 'racist' who wasn't interested in his artists; he didn't seem to realize that a more subtle approach might pay off. The avenues he went down led nowhere, only the pirate radio stations where the DJs thrived on their quirky desire to upset the status quo, responded to the recordings he had sent out. And it was these pirates who would provide the break every singer needs. Several of these stations played tracks from the album and I think the response probably surprised even them. When their listeners requested a song over and over they got in touch with the label and arranged for me to do interviews. At last, I would say to myself, finally, we were on the way. But more often than not the police would raid these pirate stations and the interview would come to nothing. It was extremely frustrating, I can tell you.

But from the outset it was clear that all wasn't doom and gloom. A friend who had the Reggae Time slot on Radio London on Sunday evenings plugged the songs like a true champion. We have remained firm friends and I am truly grateful for everything he has done for me. He liked what he had heard and he encouraged his listeners to spread the word about the album. And, encouragingly, there was always a good response. People called in week after week to hear the tracks we had laid down. But the Radio London audience was comparatively small, mainly black Londoners or those who could pick up the signal in the suburbs; the very same people who might well have heard and bought the songs at the independent outlets.

Somehow or other Capitol Radio got hold of a copy of my song. I wasn't so sure who played it first. He occupied the 4:a.m. to 6:a.m. slot and someone alerted me – I can't remember who – that the jockey was getting requests for the track on every programme. This was fantastic news. Even though I hadn't earned a penny for my work the thought that so many people appreciated my efforts sent a shiver down my spine. The fact that it was being played on mainstream radio was definitely heart-warming. That callers wanted to hear the number again and again suggested that there was an audience of more than shift workers or insomniacs interested in the song. I had no idea about the size of the audience at that early hour but, if enough of them requested it, I thought, soon it would generate some real interest.

And it did. Another friend phoned me, all breathless with excitement, at about the same time.

'Do you watch the TV a-m channel?' she asked.

'No, I don't,' I answered, for I was normally too busy getting ready for work to bother with television at that early hour.

'Well, you should,' she suggested.

'Why?' I was mildly curious.

'Your song, was on famous exercise programme this morning.'

I made a point of tuning in the next two days but, for some inexplicable reason, I didn't catch the crucial bit of the show. Damn! All that effort only to miss my song! So I set up the video before I went to work on the third day: it had to be third time lucky. If so many of my friends were in the know, why should I be the odd one out? When I returned from work there it was, ready and waiting for me. Shimmering in the background as the presenter went through her exercise routine, was my song! 'Wow!' I went, freezing on the spot as the song I had worked so hard to get right drifted over the air waves. 'My goodness!' A few days later I received an invitation to appear on the programme.

How did the programme makers get my details? What were they expecting me to do? The suddenness of the invitation caught me off guard. National television! And with so little time to prepare myself! Although I had hoped that the album would sell well and bring some reward for the months of insults and hard grind, I hadn't in my wildest dreams thought it might lead to this. Appearing on television to promote my music hadn't occurred to me. In my mind I had only gotten as far as visualizing good record sales and receiving a portion of what I was due for all those early mornings travelling to and fro.

This was on another level, but I didn't set my hopes too high. I would make the most of my guest appearance and, if that helped to drive the record it would be a bonus. But first there was my hair to do; for which black woman goes outdoors without making sure that her curls are in shape? And what should I wear? My children were as excited as I was. I could see the pleasure and pride in their young eyes. They had put up with my frequent absences and grumpiness, they had secretly wished that something would come of the long days in London and now there was an outside chance that the long days would pay off. My family phoned to wish me luck and to offer encouragement. A good show could transform our lives, they reminded me, and not in a way that made me feel under pressure but something to keep at the back of my mind.

I got up at 2 a.m. in order to get to the studio for four as had been arranged. As the taxicab the television studio had sent to collect me negotiated the quiet London streets, I tried to imagine what it would be like being on television. Some actors, newsreaders and presenters were said to be naturals, others still had the fear of freezing before the camera: which category would I fall into? I pushed all thoughts of nerves and how I might appear to the millions of homes serving breakfast out of my mind. I had fronted a band, I reminded myself, I was accustomed to audiences, I would be all right. Family and friends would be tuning in to wish me well, how could I disappoint them?

The television studio was every bit as glamorous as I had pictured it. High-ceilinged, spacious, alive with technology, it was a place where dreams collided with hard news. It was on the first floor and I distinctly recall the clarity of the sound that came from it. Stars who were household names moved confidently within its brightly-lit corridors, it was truly an introduction to another world. Dreams were created in this very building, I remember telling myself, the soaps, comedy sketches, news of wars and famine were filtered and beamed to millions of homes like servings from the same menu. I marvelled at the technology, I prayed that it would be kind to me.

Eventually I was introduced to the host of the exercise program. She was a lovely lady, kind and warm, with curly brown hair that bounced and flopped like it could defy gravity. It was a strange feeling meeting someone who was a regular on television. Tall and painfully skinny, her trait helped me to calm the slight nerves that were developing. I had been invited to appear on the show but in my excitement I hadn't asked what precisely they wanted me to do. I soon found out. The time slot in the breakfast programme was an exercise routine, I was to join her!

Exercise, strutting about, luckily I had packed a tracksuit, it might have been a new one but it could equally have been one I used for my keep-fit sessions. 'I'm sorry,' I pleaded to her gently, 'but I don't know the moves.' She couldn't be more encouraging. 'Just follow me,' she suggested, with a wink, 'you'll be fine.'

So concentrating with all my might, I joined the gentle work out, albeit lagging by a few steps, with my song playing in the background.

Too busy focusing on keeping time I didn't have time to worry about being on television. What I was doing seemed natural; I had no fear of being under the spotlight. At the end of the show, she congratulated me and gave me a hug. Our routine had gone well, would I be prepared to do two more? Would I indeed! Who in their right mind would turn down such an opportunity?

I was told that the switchboard was jammed after my appearance. Viewers wanted to know everything about me; they wanted to know where they could get the record. They had now linked the voice and face, it was more than a song to be played as you stretched and limbered up before setting out for a day at the office or factory. Thousands wanted a copy. Television had sprinkled its magic for me, I had to seize the opportunity. This letter, part of which is reproduced below, was typical of the reaction to the programme.

Dear Elizabeth,
You have been playing [a] lovely record, which my daughter and family love very much. Please, do you

think the singer has made a video of it? If no can you give me the name of the singer and record company?

The record exploded, that's the only way to describe it. It was like a power surge, connecting people and towns across the length and breadth of the UK. Fans appeared in the most unlikely towns and villages; my unusual name was on their lips. Those who regularly joined the exercise routine splashed out on the record they had grown to love, so much so that on my next appearance I was presented with a silver disc.

Behind the scenes my producer had responded like a man who has punched for a modest 30 pounds at a cashpoint machine and suddenly finds hundreds of notes of all denominations floating into his grateful lap. With the demand for the record at such a height the distributors he had sought were now contacting him. The grey 1986 record label credits both him and the arranger, the multi-talented musician; my name is there in bold, as is that of the distributor. The public wanted a copy of the disc, demanded it even, it was simply a case of meeting the demand. Within a fortnight the sales had totaled more than a cool quarter of a million.

And so now to the matter of contracts, I had begun the studio recordings in good faith, determined to give life to the songs, my composer had worked so hard to compose and assuming that the record label owner saw us as partners, singer, arranger and producer. The label was owned by a black man, the producer would be fair, wouldn't he? Composer, singer, arranger, producer, engineer, each played a critical role in the birth of a disc. It would have been naive to expect an equal split, but, as I returned home after a session and prepared for the next, I was confident that since we were all West Indians and were plugging Caribbean music, this common bond would be enough to see us over our little disagreements.

When the contract eventually arrived I didn't know what to make of the 18 page document. I had never seen singing as a way of making a fortune, but equally when I totalled the hours I had committed to the project an album invariably is, the contract felt like a slap in the face: it wasn't simply an insult, it was exploitation.

It was a generic contract with my name handwritten into the blank spaces. It had obviously been drawn up for a previous male artist, for I was referred to as 'he' and 'his' throughout. After numerous paragraphs of legal and technical jargon I could barely follow, my eyes fixed themselves to page eleven. This outlined the royalties I was to agree to, and I was horrified.

On record sales in the UK, the document stated, I was to receive 5% in the first year of recording, 6% in the second, rising by a single percentage point each year until, in the fifth year, I would be awarded 9%. For sales in the rest of the world, the royalties would begin at 2.5% in the first year and increase by 0.5% annually until the fifth year to 4.5%. As an illustration, according to a Royalty Statement from the record company, from the 1st July 1987 to 31 December 1987, UK sales for our second single totalled 143 428. The royalties earned amounted to £7104. 91. During the same period, the follow-up up single sold 93 525 copies. My earnings from this were £5193.85. I received a total of £12,299 for sales of just under £220 000!

I won't go into the details about the sales for the first half of that year. All I would state is that from January to June various records sold a total of £281 882 and that I received just under £14,000. The contract is dated 1 August 1985. The first of August is Emancipation Day in the British Caribbean, celebrating the overthrow of the odious slave system. The irony would have been lost on the record producer.

Singers like myself, new to the industry, put their trust in those they work with but having looked at the section outlining what I was to be paid, it was clear that this contract was too heavily biased in favour of the owner of the label. I had pushed myself hard, had made the trip to London when others were having their Sunday lunch, had dug deep to do justice to his creations. Had he forgotten the success of our first single which was number one in the reggae charts for weeks? And to be rewarded so pitifully? Is that how he treated all his artists, or was it just me?

There were solicitors specializing in music contracts I would learn later, but I discovered they charged thousands just to read a contract. I was a divorcee with two children and a home to maintain, hundreds would have stretched my funds; that kind of money would have been way out of my range. If it cost that much just to read, what would it have cost to negotiate and amend a contract that was so blatantly unjust?

Having gone through these grim thoughts in my mind, in the end I took the contract I had been sent by the label owner to a firm of solicitors. Solicitors were experts, I said to myself, after years of academic study and legal practice they would be able to spot and advise on such a glaring injustice. One of the partners took a cursory look at the contract then pronounced, 'It seems all right.' He wasn't an expert in music contracts, he had explained, but I was expecting him to use his knowledge of contracts in general to come to a professional judgement. 'The contract's fine,' he repeated when he saw the look of astonishment on my face. So, lacking the funds to pursue the matter and out of options, I signed a contract that credited me with 5% pence per single in the UK instead of the customary 24 pence, as I would later discover.

CHAPTER ELEVEN

Publicity

BUT I WASN'T THINKING OF contracts when the record exploded. I was in demand and any opportunity that came my way had to be seized. You get one chance in life is the cliché, but how true it is. If you fail to recognize it you might end up holding your head in your hands or banging that same head against a wall for missing the boat. As the sales rocketed more and more people contacted the label and the producer passed on my details. It was a strange but exhilarating feeling, taking calls from people who had big-time connections and proper clout. I was a 'star', a 'sensation', they all assured me when they took me to lunch or dinner, the public was clamouring for a piece of me. I was a star, but one with barely a penny coming her way.

A television network was one of the first to get in touch. It wanted to do a programme about me, the producer said. I was young, attractive, good television fare. They didn't say this to me directly but the message behind their invitation wasn't hard to decipher. Viewers loved the idea of an ordinary young woman 'hitting the big time', movies offered the dream, the small screen wasn't going to be left behind. Londoners would get to see another 'rags to riches' tale and who was I to disappoint viewers as they took their meal?

A young woman from the Caribbean, 'exotic', with an unusual route to the top, what better story to feed the public? Being a star with a hit record, the TV company suggested that viewers would be switching on in droves to get a glimpse into the high life I was now getting accustomed to. They were prepared to follow me on one of my shopping trips, the broadcast was bound to draw in millions.

Where do we draw the line between reality and what the public expects? Does such a line exist, and should we worry about it? Was it fair to pretend that I was partying and clubbing and drinking champagne every night of the week when, in reality, the struggle to meet the mortgage was constantly at the back of my mind? The questions are academic now, but at the time I must say it was a weird feeling living these two conflicting lives. The director wasn't interested in my true existence: I was selling hundreds of thousands of records so I had to be a pop star. Simple as that. And since I was a star, I had to live like a celebrity, I deserved it! This was the version of events that would hold their public.

For the male English pop star, the stereotype was probably drink and drugs, for a Caribbean woman, glamour, shopping on a grand scale, sex, with a battery of suitors waiting in the wings. I was attractive, dressed well, I had a good figure, the image I had to portray was of a woman who had left behind a life of drudgery and now moved in elevated circles of rich, sophisticated men and women. So there we were in London with me buying and parading all these expensive dresses I couldn't afford, posing for the camera, acting out the star, pretending that mine was a life of parties and champagne, when I was practically broke! All champagne and no knickers, as the English say!

They would feed the public the simple storyline it craved, the television company promised, although they weren't that blatant about it. And, even if I didn't think of it at the time, looking back, it made perfect sense. Broadcasting likes to peddle the 'girl or woman who had made it' story, and who was a more worthy candidate for Cinderella? A 'factory girl' one day, a 'superstar' the next, could there be a better fantasy?

I had transferred from the lighting company to a medical instruments company. To fill in the background to my life, to add another layer to their story, a television crew turned up to interview my work colleagues. That extra little touch for the viewers, you see. I would be captured at my previous day job, looking ordinary, to add that rich contrast to the glamour that now surrounded me. They spent the day filming and talking to my friends, searching for that little nugget to add spice to the programme. Fame hadn't gone to my head, my colleagues happily confirmed, I was the same woman; there were no airs and graces. What they didn't know, television crew and co-workers, was that I was relying on the wages from the medical instruments company I was working for that time to play the star for the media.

This was also the era when the music video was coming into its own. Television appearances weren't enough for the viewing public they wanted their own slice of you, a video they could play at their leisure. Slide the VHS cassette into the recorder, press Play, and sit back with a drink and something to nibble on: tea or coffee, or something stronger, and perhaps a takeaway pizza. It made sense, I suppose, 'home entertainment' was giving viewers and listeners the freedom and choice that would explode with DVDs and mobiles. Fans wanted their personal copy of singer and music, and with a director engaged, I set about trying to please them.

I had seen music videos of course, but I had no idea of the amount of work involved. In the most popular ones, a singer paraded in some exotic location, trying to look casual, classy and cool. Some white sandy beach, perhaps, or some exclusive boutique where price was no object. Fast luxurious cars took her from one location to the next; the camera captured these slices of her fantastic story and processed it as the life that awaited the legions of would be stars, eager for an opportunity to shine. Now that I was a part of the 'dream industry' I threw myself in wholeheartedly, for I wasn't one for half measures. The video company wanted to capture the heart and soul of the hit, I was happy to defer to their judgement.

They had listened carefully to the song, I'll give them that. Having to choose between two lovers, I was in torment (in the song that is). I don't know how they did it but they managed to convey the message of the hit without it sounding corny or looking overdone. The video they produced is just over three minutes long, skilfully edited, and still looks fresh after 25 years. The set was a club and restaurant, and the location beautifully summed up the soul-searching at the heart of the song.

My daughter had a small part in the video. A Vincentian dancer, who had performed with Kylie Minogue and other international artists, played my beau. His cousin worked with me at the medical instruments company. With his good looks and easy charm, curly perm and rich moustache, he took to the role like the professional dancer and actor he was. Suave, sophisticated, and definitely younger than me, he could well have been the aching lover I wanted to be with in the song. It was an eye-opening experience for me, a glimpse into a world fantastic and tempting with just enough reality to make sure you kept your feet on firm ground.

Dressed in a gold figure-hugging dress, in the video I descend the gentle left-winding stairs clinging to my steady love and into the heart of a sophisticated club where my admirer waits patiently. My other brother is one of the crowds. My daughter, 17 at the time and also getting into the role, is relaxing at the bar with a man at least twice her age nursing a glass of orange juice, pretending that this is where she normally spends her evenings. Watching the video again I can see that she has a distant look. What is she thinking, I wonder? That she should be at home revising for her A' levels?

As the story unfolds, I detach myself from my old love and join the three-piece band, singing a verse to the camera. Then, slowly, shyly, I saunter to the table where my new love longs for me to join him. We are soon at the bar, and he takes my hand and caresses my fingers while I sing to him. He kisses my hand, one, twice, it is very romantic. This guy plays the aching lover to perfection, that wistful look in his eyes, young, but already aware of the cold acceptance that unless we are brave and ruthless our lives are not our own, but often at the direction of others.

As I make to leave with the partner I arrived with, he takes my hand in one last desperate plea for us to be together. But, recognizing the hopelessness of his devotion, he allows it to slide slowly away. I waltz up the stairs, but by the time I'm half way up, I'm racing like you do when your dress is too tight or your heels too high and you feel you might lose your balance at any moment.

All the 'extras' contributed to the simple story, and I must say the director got the best out of us. Ten hours of filming reduced to a mere three minutes and 46 seconds on video: it was the stuff of dreams: looking at it now it was a wonderful experience; I wonder what viewers made of it. All those, 'takes', getting the mood just right, I'm sure they had no idea of the amount of time we had spent filming.

With my popularity at its height, the local papers weren't going to miss out on the action. I didn't belong to the nation they seemed to imply, I was a Dickson 'girl' first and foremost. No matter that they only printed negative stories of West Indians or ignored us completely, the town had nurtured me. If I hit the big time it was thanks in some way to its careful handling. The clippings I have kept show me smiling hugely for every newspaper and in elegant poses, some sexy, others simply weary, although it's only noticeable if you look closely. Almost all the articles refer to me as a 'factory girl' on an assembly line, as though I was fitting the engine on a car or something similar in a heavy industrial plant churning out thousands of vehicles a day.

After the local press to the county ones, from all parts of Bucks, reporters rolled up following in the footsteps of some of the national press, all searching for some fresh angle to sell their papers. What they found was DD, an ordinary Caribbean woman, although from the way they spun it, I was right up there with the top stars living the good life. They wrote that my children were carting handfuls of autographed photos to school, but that I had remained a normal Mom who still did her shopping. Looking for the best buys at the supermarket one day, appearing in front of an audience of 10 million the next; that was the portrayal one paper came up with. My life was 'ambivalent', one reported, but I took all the trappings of success in my stride.

Another paper revealed that I loved soaps, especially Cheers. Apparently, I had it hot for the barman in the programme. The tabloids are chiefly out to tantalize their readers. If they can't have the sordid details of a story, if alcohol, sex, glamour or a tangled life doesn't come up to scratch, they dig for a love angle. They pushed and pushed until I revealed that, yes, I had a new sweetheart. I wouldn't reveal his name, the published article added, because he was shy. My 'shy boyfriend' took me out for meals regularly, the piece continued, Indian or Chinese food were our favourites.

But, at least one of the clippings I have in front of me got it right: I was into keep-fit big time to stay healthy and to keep my figure trim: after all the fancy meals and late nights I was supposed to be enjoying in the restaurants, I would have needed to exercise twice a day, if not three! Surprisingly, as I see from a cutting from one of the other papers, I enjoyed cooking coq-au-vin! No mention of rice and peas or pelau, they must have thought I was a prime example of a West Indian woman who had embraced the English life. I did gardening for relaxation, the same piece written, wasn't I the very epitome of the Caribbean woman who represented the best in old Blighty?

The joys of stardom! I was, according to yet another of these publications, 'Britain's best kept secret'. The lovely Caribbean lady with the seductive voice who had captured the nation's hearts, was the picture they painted of me. One tantalizing spot away from the top slot in the charts, only the Queen of Pop, Madonna, could hold me off, it wrote. All reporters wished me luck in the quest for the number one position, their paper was behind me, they were keen to make clear.

The song spent five weeks at number two. After the expectation of the first two it felt like knocking at a locked door, shoving it with the shoulders, twisting the handle, applying every conceivable force, but lacking the one thing that would work: the key. But being pipped by a singer with a following in countries I would never penetrate was no shame or disgrace. Never mind, I told myself, never mind, indeed. According to the local papers I still had my holidays to look forward to; second place behind a woman with an established publicity machine at her disposal was an achievement in itself. The city touched me deeply, I allegedly told the reporter, the narrow winding roads reminded me of my childhood.

Inevitably, some of the papers delved deeper into my background. They were after some new angle, something salacious for their readers. Thank goodness there weren't a thousand television and radio channels then with more and more niche markets to satisfy. Now that each outlet has to offer something 'fresh' or outrageous to its viewers, I dread to think of the mess they would have made of my previous life. One national paper reported that my ex-husband was being plagued by voodoo dolls in a mental home. How they came by that snippet I never discovered, I'm just thankful that they didn't probe further. In answer to one question, perhaps not fully realizing how the press might spin it, I apparently told some reporter that my marriage had been a tragedy. Did I really say that?

The marriage had brought us both heartbreaks, the same paper printed, but what occurred was due to the unlucky hand dealt us by fate. I can remember saying something similar, and I still stand by that statement. There was no question of infidelity or falling out of love, I told them as succinctly as I could, my husband had changed into a person beyond his control.

The paper printed my comments on my failed marriage accurately, I wanted the world to know a little of what I had been through so that they wouldn't see a shallow starlet, chasing fame at all costs. I hoped that they could see through some of the hype, could recognize me as a Caribbean woman juggling the demands of home, work and a career. And even if I was being feted and dined and enjoying the razzmatazz of the record business, didn't I deserve some success for all the struggles and strife?

But I wasn't reaping the rewards of my success. I had signed away my right to a decent share of the profit from my recordings that others raked it in. I attended all the promotional events lined up for me, performed, smiled and said not a bad word; that wasn't the kind of person I was. I wasn't going to publicly slate the people who had helped me along the road. But it hurt, it really did. Sales were phenomenal for both songs, enough to warrant appearances on Top of the Pops. Even now the interest in them is still strong, as can be seen from the number of hits on the internet. My song was at number two for five weeks in 1987, but was I a millionairess living in some secluded spot in an exclusive island for the rich, as some people imagined?

CHAPTER TWELVE

National Television

SO THE RECORD EXPLODED. THE song that had cost me so much in hurt pride and effort had become the surprise hit in early 1987. Congratulations poured in; everywhere I went the Caribbean community was delighted for me. If a West Indian appeared on national television for some notoriety we all felt ashamed, when they were feted for some prestigious achievement we beamed with pride. And so it was with me on the success of my records. You could see the lift it gave some people; my story was one they could readily identify with.

Some knew what I had been through, both with my husband and in an effort to get a fair return on the records, so they were especially pleased that the song had rocketed up the Top Thirty. In knowledge or in ignorance, all those who took the trouble to phone guessed that chart success wasn't the same thing as raking in a personal fortune. Local people still saw me at the market or shopping in town, I wasn't in any way elusive. I made sure that I kept up with all the social events in the Caribbean calendar. A stranger in the city would have had no trouble finding my address.

Bob Marley and the Wailers, Dennis Brown, Bob Andy and Marcia Griffiths, Gregory Isaacs, Aswad, John Holt, UB 40, and a host of other singers and groups had had good runs in the charts but, I've since been told, I was the first solo female Caribbean singer to score a hit in the British charts since the last time. That might have been true and if it was, the satisfaction the person who told me hoped this would bring was tinged with a dash of sadness. All the wonderful music Caribbean artists had made over the years – calypso, soca and reggae – to think that the British public hadn't had the opportunity to hear but a tiny proportion of them! To think that some of these great singers went unrecognized and unrewarded! What a waste of talent!

I didn't see myself as a trendsetter or anything like that. I was a relative novice to the music business and I had had my struggles to get this record out. There had been no discussion of a follow-up album, where I went after the publicity dried up was a question I was too scared to ask myself because I dreaded the answer. One-hit wonders were two-a-penny, who was to say that I wouldn't join their ranks? Those who believed I was raking in thousands were cruelly mistaken: I hadn't seen anything like the sums people imagined despite 'crossing over'. But I had secured an agent to represent me, and I had a gut feeling that somewhere along the road I would get the bookings I needed to help with my rapidly declining finances.

With the record sitting pretty in the national charts at number two, an appearance was arranged for Top of the Pops. When the invitation came, I was over the moon; for how else could I describe that initial sensation? The rush of fame, the thrill of being recognized. I would be lying if I said I didn't enjoy the light-headed feeling that followed the request to go on the national show. You hear of people walking round in a stupor or feeling as though they are floating on air … well, I was like that for two days. As I prepared myself mentally for what was to be my debut, I thought back to my time with my first band and how far I had travelled musically.

The band could almost have been of a different era, it occurred to me, as the day of the broadcast approached. During the dozens of small but essential things I had to do before the big day itself, I cast my mind back to the evenings when the family would sit in front of our old black and white television, mesmerized by the grace and elegance of the American soul stars. Aretha Franklin, Otis Redding, Sam Cooke, wasn't there something magical about the names, we would say to one another? Didn't the names sound big, bold, magical, didn't they trip off the tongue as though each singer could never have been called by any other name?

I would gasp like a child at their outfits and marvel at the way each performer bent the voice to give meaning to words we used every day to reassure a loved one or to call a halt to an up and down relationship. An extra syllable blended into a word of adoration, or a quickening of a phrase, how sweetly they pleasured the ears! The control my heroes held over a song couldn't fail to instil a sense of awe in someone like myself just starting out. They were the height of glamour, supreme in every way, and now I was about to project myself to the glare and scrutiny of a new public, but without their years of experience.

A sway, a demure shift of the head from the camera: everything my heroes did seemed so natural it was as if, for an instant, I could snatch a glimpse into the soul of a true star. Some of these artists had subsequently come to England and now, probably in the very studio where they had performed on of their fabulous hits, I was about to appear and have my image beamed to the millions enjoying the warm English spring! Somewhere among the viewers the programme attracted, might there be a young singer observing me closely, in the same way I had fixed on my American heroes?

Well-wishers phoned daily; they sounded as excited as when I had first appeared on Breakfast TV. Scores of calls came, all pledging their support. I thanked each person sincerely, for I knew that West Indians like to see one of their own thrive. When it truly matters, we are able to cast aside our petty differences. Our bosoms swell with pride when our people shine on the international stage. Our cricketers were world champions at the time, and we walked around with our chests puffed out when they thrashed the opposition from

Australia, India, Pakistan and, yes, England too. As with sport so with music, I hoped.

When the day finally came my family tried to behave as though this was a commonplace event to take in their stride. But I knew that deep down they were praying for me. They had watched me struggle to get my life back; they had kept my secrets deep in their bosoms. Now they set up the video recorder so that we could enjoy the result in the comfort of home. The SVG High Commission in London had gotten in touch. They promised to spread the news to Vincentians throughout the country. Our countrymen and women would have elbowed a reminder to their friends, the embassy added, as if I needed reminding. Caribbean people the length and width of Britain would be wishing me well: I had no intention of disappointing them.

I caught the train to London on the day of the recording. I had secured a Personal Assistant, and she travelled with me, taking care of all the minor details, leaving me free to focus on my performance. She was a wonderful lady, supportive, professional, what I would have done without her I dread to think. The hairdressers had been booked, that was our first port of call and they did a superb job. No matter how my times I replay the video I am still astonished at the craftsmanship of that salon. The four hours or so it took to style my hair was time and money well spent.

My hair had been cut short for my debut and fully tapered at the back. But it was still black and luscious, full and tantalizing. For my second appearance on the show I sported a pageboy look, feathered at the front, and, I must say, the professionalism and artistry of the hairdressers and beauticians couldn't be faulted then either. Personal appearance was every bit as important as the song itself, the staff nudged me as they applied the finishing touches, to dampen the effect of an expensive dress with my hair a-tangle would have been insane.

For my debut I wore a blue Chinese style jacket with a closed neck and three buttons and black parachute pants. Watching the video now the outfit was a hit, as was the costume jewellery. On the second show I sported a cream bolero top with a leg of lamb sleeve over a puffball cream skirt, another hit, I'm not ashamed to say. The costumes were bought at a famous bazaar along with three or four other dresses which, I'm happy to report, I still have today. They're slight tight in a few places but, if take a deep breath and forget to exhale for five minutes or so, I can still climb into them!

Everyone accepted that Top of the Pops was an 'institution'. A single appearance could launch an artist, the programme could almost grow a career out of brown straw. Success in the reggae charts was gratifying, but, in the final reckoning it was small scale; it was like scoring a four in cricket, not smashing a mighty six clean out the park. The opportunity to launch myself on the British stage was now within my grasp, how could I not go all out for it?

I made every effort to dress well, to present myself in the best possible light. West Indian women throughout the country would be glued to the television set, I was aware, analyzing and scrutinizing everything. Some British viewers also made a hobby of searching for anachronisms or anything the least bit out of place, they were just as hard to please. An ill-fitting dress, clashing colours,

mascara or rouge badly applied: the lines to the BBC would be jammed: I had no intention of being the subject of complaints in one form or another.

The BBC studio, has acquired legendary status. It was the home of thousands of ground-breaking transmissions. News and light entertainment flowed from it to all corners of the globe like sun rays darting unbendingly to their distant destinations. On each appearance at the historic studio I was accorded the treatment star performers received. I was ushered into a spacious dressing room with make-up artists to ensure that I projected the image I wanted. There were soft drinks and a hearty lunch in the famous BBC canteen. I don't recall being nervous, I'm fortunate that I'm one of those people who can get up on stage and perform without the self-consciousness that attacks others in the business.

Apart from delivering the song what was expected? How should I project myself? Performers didn't receive much by way of instructions from the programme makers. Well, not as much as I had expected. No great technical stuff about lighting or sound, no tips about how to look our best. They didn't explain what they hoped the final product would look like, I was to get onto the stage and sing.

Perhaps the producer thought that we were professionals accustomed to the medium of television, perhaps image wasn't as important then as it is now. Whatever the reason the guidance was pretty basic; performers shouldn't wear black, we shouldn't wear shiny clothes. And finally, as I was about to mount the stage, I was informed that at all times, I should face the camera with the red light.

The studio where the filming took place was small. Television managed to make it seem vast. As the cameras swept along the audience it was easy to believe that the recording was done in front of hundreds. In reality we were working within quite a confined space. The audience was brought in for effect, there wasn't the energy that a live crowd creates.

Taking these considerations into account, all three of my appearances seemed smooth and self-assured. In the two minutes and thirty-two seconds of the first broadcast there is no hint of nervousness; the performance is polished as if I had been doing it all my life. I gave off a confident aura in all three appearances, if that's not too boastful. From the videos or the links on you tube there is emotion in the performances as well as delivery. Even the dry ice they had warned me about didn't faze me: as the fog seeped onto the stage for dramatic effect I simply ignored it and laid into the song. The audience they had brought into the cramped studio – to lend authenticity to the show – responded enthusiastically, and I left the stage with a real feeling of euphoria. I had done it, I had appeared on Top of The Pops!

Artists were escorted back to the dressing room after their performances and I must say I felt quite elated. How long it took to get down from that high I couldn't tell. There hadn't been a single hitch that I could think of, I just hoped that the broadcast would convey the quiet pleasure I felt inside. I thought of my Mom, my children, watching at home, of my siblings, and of the other band members who were willing me on. Those thousands of Vincentians and other Caribbean people cheering for me; I could almost hear and see them,; that open Caribbean smile adorning their faces. My PA was happy, all our meticulous preparations had paid off and if she said it had gone well, who was I to disagree?

Who were the other artists on the bill during the three shows? I'm ashamed to say that I can't remember. The singers didn't mingle as I had expected. I had imagined us all lunching together, swapping stories and cheering each other on. Instead, safe in our dressing rooms we were too busy getting ready to give time to socializing or supporting the other acts. Similarly, I had thought that we would bump into some of the household names, people who adorned our television. That didn't happen either, except for one. As we were leaving the studios in the taxi the BBC had provided to take us home, I recall seeing a famous personality that time just entering. He was hot property at the time, the darling of British television. What was even more satisfying than seeing a famous face was the throng of fans at the gate chanting, 'DD' as our taxi pulled away.

I had made my mark in the UK so it was time to spread my wings. But where to? I understand that an American producer had tried to license the record over there but that my record label owner had refused. What a missed opportunity. Never mind, there were other countries where people had fallen in love with my song.

Before my involvement in the music industry I didn't realize that there was another market in Europe waiting to be tapped. As the song reverberated throughout country after country, promoters bought it under license and so off I scurried to promote it.

This was my first trip on the continent. In fact it would be an exaggeration to say that that I had travelled far and wide since my arrival in England nearly 20 years earlier. I didn't know what kind of reception to expect but I was determined not only to repay those who had paid for my flight and accommodation with all the professionalism I always gave to a performance. I was doubly keen to see those countries that were keen to see me.

At the time, my daughter was in the final year of her A' levels and, being an independent young girl, she encouraged me to go. She could cope with her studies, she assured me, I wasn't to worry. My son I was a bit more concerned about. It was unfair to expect Mom to look after him or them both. My mother was getting on, she had to look after herself. In the end I booked him into a boarding school and I can distinctly remember how reluctant and angry he was. 'You don't love me,' he yelped, 'I don't want to go.' But I sat him down and explained the position; it was an opportunity I couldn't turn down, I told him, he might understand my position when he was older.

Germany was the first country I went to and it was a revelation. I had imagined it as cold, harsh and regimental, the home of the prestigious BMW and Mercedes. Precise and dour, that was how I thought of the people. The idea that thousands would turn up to see me perform would have made me chuckle with disbelief a few months earlier. But they were there, singing along to my songs, showing a side that smile with happiness. In Frankfurt, I stayed in the top hotels, I luxuriated in the treatment I received on this, my first tour.

My road manager sorted the day-to-day affairs, he made sure that the backing tapes were at hand, arranged sound checks, all the minor details that have to be in place before a show. All I had to do was to sing. And I did, with all the emotion and gratefulness I could muster. They heard me lament having two lovers, they applauded when I dreamt of the beautiful islands of the Caribbean, I wondered how many of them had visited them. The audiences took me to their hearts, if appearing on Top of the Pops and television networks had been unreal; performing for a foreign audience gave me a thrill like no other.

I gave my all, sang with all my might. With such lavish treatment I would have been mean-spirited not to reciprocate. The audience called out for me in their thousands, and I like to think I rose with each performance and rewarded them accordingly. From Germany I travelled to Spain. And here, for the first time on stage, after a rousing reception everywhere I went, after the demand for a repeat performance at every venue, I was lost for words. But not in the way you might imagine.

As in Germany the venues lined up for me were unlike any I had played in England. These were massive arenas, exclusive, with no expense spared in their décor. As I relaxed in my hotel rooms, I had to pinch myself at times. Was that really me up there? Was I the same girl who had had such a terrible time before, who had felt the cold gnawing at her bones during her first winter in England; who had had the reins of her life snatched from her when the man she loved became mentally ill; who had struggled for five years under a mountain of debt; who had almost been reduced to a child by a producer who was now reaping the benefits of her labour?

One night, then, at a club, a gold-plated affair like no other, there might have been a Viking theme, I'm not sure. Imagine the scene then, scores of strapping Vikings, tall, blond, as imposing as in the movies. It's a gorgeous night, the crowd receptive, noisy, happy, drinks flowing, everyone having a good time. I'm onstage singing away, swaying gently as I normally do for my act is not raunchy and thrusting. As I'm in the middle of this number one of the Vikings approached the stage.

A magnificent being, he saunters over, comes closer and closer. What does he want? Is he going to request a favourite song? I'm not worried about my security. Charged with the pleasure of performing I'm happy, in the zone as they say, making sure I don't get complacent or stale. The idea that the man might hurt me is far from my mind. I carry on singing, smiling gently at the enormous figure now a few feet away.

The song moves on, he is now close enough for me to hear him. Nobody thinks of calling him away, no one has thought that he might put me off my stride or make me feel uncomfortable. I flow with the music, keeping one eye on the audience and the other on my 'companion'. With an enormous smile on his face this mountain of a man leans over and whispers in my ear, with an enormous grin, 'DD, you are so beautiful, I would like to f….. you.' For an instant I stood there open-mouthed. He had delivered his message and that was the last I saw of him. I'm not sure if the audience saw the shock on my face. It took a good few moments for me to regain a measure of composure.

Because of the problems with my record company it would be easy to regard my time in Europe as an unhappy one. But that would be an insult to all those who worked so hard to welcome me and to make me feel at home. I stayed in the most fabulous hotels, the staff couldn't be more accommodating. In Belgium I had a whole suite to myself, every country gave me the full star treatment. As the British representative at the summer fair in Germany I was due to sing two three-minute songs but the audience had me going for over 20 minutes. When people are so kind and generous how else can you repay them but by giving your all?

I enjoyed the tours to Europe to plug the record and my appearances in Dubai and Abu Dhabi a year later were every bit as enjoyable. These were more lucrative also, but they too were an eye-opener. From the outset I discovered here also, the kindness of those who had booked me and the public took me to their hearts after my performances.

For the shows in Abu Dhabi I bought myself a new wardrobe of long dresses. I didn't wish to disrespect my hosts by appearing too 'western' in a country with a strict dress code. In temperatures approaching 100 degrees I sat in my hotel room and in restaurants with my hosts feeling restless and uncomfortable, sweat pouring off me, down me and out of sight. What a sight I must have been! I tried to act normal, making small talk with my sponsor, but it was a struggle.

My sponsor was a wonderful lady, carefully attired, cool and resplendent no matter what the time of day. Why are you dressed like that, she eventually asked, barely able to resist a smile? I explained that it was a mark of respect for the customs of the country. My sponsor broke into a hearty laugh. I can still recall her chuckling like someone who has caught you with lipstick smeared under your nose like a red moustache. 'You cover up in public,' she advised me, with an expansive wave of the hand, 'but inside you can dress as you please.'

She owned a boutique in a shopping complex not far away from where I was staying. 'Go and help yourself,' she suggested. 'Go on.'

I didn't know what to make of her suggestion. Accompanied by my friend who was my companion on the trip, I went to the shop she had described. It was a fabulous place, stylish, elegant, almost an Aladdin's cave, if I can call it that. We selected a few outfits we thought cool enough for the intense heat, but careful not to pick anything too expensive in case the costs were deducted from my performance fees. Imagine my surprise when my host told us that the dresses were complimentary!

Those were fabulous times. The reception I received in Europe and in the Middle East will live with me till the day I die. I was treated as a star, and I like to think that I gave of my best on every occasion. I was representing England, I was an ambassador for the Caribbean, and I left these countries feeling that I had given them something to remember.

CHAPTER THIRTEEN

Returning home

I LEFT FOR ENGLAND AND didn't return to SVG for over 20 years. During that time, I saw members of my family go and when they returned I listened to their breathless accounts of how the country had developed. Friends too said the same thing, and of all the Caribbean countries, no matter which one they were from. All got excited about going 'home', there was always this sense of anticipation as the day of departure drew near. Such was the pull of the islands that for many it was difficult to get them to talk of anything else once they had booked their passage and received the precious tickets in the post.

Sunshine and sea were calling them, they joked. There was nothing to beat a diet of fresh fish, coconut water, juicy plumrose and mangoes, and provisions fresh from the ground. Music and nightlife lit up the place for those who were into such things, they said, you could stroll anywhere with a freedom unimaginable in England, if you fancied a quieter experience. Invariably after their holiday in the sun, almost everyone I knew came back to England feeling and looking sad and miserable; not because of some dreadful calamity, it soon became clear, theirs was the pain of lovers having to say au revoir to their dearest. On my first trip back, I was to taste some of that pain.

Why did it take me so long, I ask myself now that I've settled back in the Caribbean? What had prevented me making the journey? How come I hadn't felt the pull of the Caribbean so many in our community talked of daily, like people who cannot help living in the past?

Circumstances, I suppose, I simply wasn't in a position to undertake such a trip. I fell pregnant at 19 and, as a single parent - although I didn't see myself as such - I had to devote myself to bringing up my daughter. My marriage soon after then became my priority, there was a house to run and children to look after. My husband's declining mental health didn't allow time to think about much else, it consumed my every long day and fretful night. The mountain of debt I faced after the divorce meant that what is quite an expensive holiday-typically eight hundred pounds - was out of the question. Now, finally, with a couple of hit records behind me and the children grown-up, after 22 years, I was to visit the country I left at 15.

There was an organization in SVG, a band of which the singer became an international star, another in the list of talented performers SVG has produced. I was informed that I had made a name for myself in Europe, would I like to appear as the star performer? Naturally, I accepted the invitation. It's always an honour to be asked to appear as a guest. I didn't see the offer as an opportunity for promotion but it was more a case of giving back something to the island that had looked after me during my early childhood, and having the kind of holiday my friends and family boasted about.

I had left the country with a slight sadness in my heart, but I was excited at the thought of returning. I saw the visit as a chance to perform, to see my Vincentian relatives again, and to bask in the sunshine which I love dearly. To be truthful I had no real idea about what Vincentians had made of the record: the radio stations plugged it out of a sense of loyalty, I imagined, their listeners were proud that a fellow Vincentian had appeared in the British charts. But beyond that, before the invitation from the Young Turks, I had had little feedback. I saw myself doing the show, meeting the local musicians and singers, getting in some sun, sea and sight-seeing, then flying back to England with my batteries recharged and on the right-hand side of the scale.

But first there was the problem of where to stay. I didn't want to be accused of being uppity like those West Indians who return to the Caribbean and spend their entire holiday in some fancy hotel because they feel ashamed of their village, or shudder with shame when confronted with the rude house in which they grew up. It seemed ridiculous to me to shut away or disown what had been a part of my young life. My family was in Dickson, I was proud to be associated with them, my childhood memories there had been happy ones, so that was the first place to come to mind.

But I had to be pragmatic. Despite my wish to be treated as just another family member, I recognized that there might be a practical problem: I was travelling with my partner, the house had accommodated us when we were children but how would it cope with two more adults? I wrote to my sister, for advice. I wanted to come and spend time with her and her family, I said in my letter, would that be all right?

A part of me tells me that she was slightly anxious that the house might not come up to the standard she imagined of our homes in England; perhaps she simply recognized that there wasn't enough space for another person, much less two. Whichever it was, she suggested that it might be better to stay in town, or with my aunts'. In a way I had expected her to explain that her house was quite basic, that we would miss the comforts of England, but what surprised me was the suggestion that I contact my aunt.

At the mention of my aunts', some of the old memories blazed back: the domestic chores, the silence, and the night when I thought my time was up. But the years had rolled on, I reminded myself, I had managed to get over the uneasiness I felt in that household. I was a married woman with a family, my aunt would be nearing 60, and her children would be adults. She probably didn't realize the extent of my unhappiness when I dwelled with her, but I didn't hold any grudges or bad feelings. So why not get in touch, I asked myself?

St. Vincent and Dominica are the two Windward Islands without an international airport. As I write, Argyle International is under construction in SVG and for Vincentians worldwide the day cannot come too soon when it is finished. Cheaper fares - hopefully - a direct flight from Gatwick landing you there in time to catch a dip in the sea or a short afternoon nap to rest the weary bones: what a joy that would be!

Back then, in November 1987, it was an eight-hour flight on Virgin Atlantic or British Airways to Grantley Adams International in Barbados, a stopover that lasted anything from two hours to seven, then a short hop 'home'. In extreme cases, passengers had to sleep at the airport and catch the early flight a day later.

And something similar was in store for me, much to my frustration. The flight from London was delayed so we missed our early-evening connection. Twenty –

two years, an eight-hour journey, and 100 miles of Caribbean Sea still separated me from 'home'. But I had learned patience, people from SVG have had years of practice at it and I was no different. Besides, the hotel in Barbados went some way to make up for the frustration. Sam Lords was a delightful place, it certainly lived up to its reputation for comfort and service.

Early the following morning, I finally climbed aboard a plane for the 40-minute flight to St Vincent. The plane climbed steadily then headed west; the 30 or so passengers from England or North America all tired and grateful to be within touching distance of 'home'. As the aircraft made its final descent into the airport, I looked out the window and said a silent prayer of thanks. Finally, after a day and a half travelling, the cabin door opened and I felt the rush of hot air that announces that you've arrived in the Caribbean.

The blast of hot air took me by surprise, but there was an even greater shock waiting for me as I descended. There was a tremendous crowd waiting to welcome me home! I was too overawed to take proper count. My sister and her family were there and she broke down with emotion. I was tearful too, as you can imagine; after 22 years apart there was so much catching up to do. Some members of the Young Turks had also turned out to welcome me. The attorney-general that time, representing the government, was as dignified as ever in his official greeting. He would later arrange a motorcade from with the SVG News reporter in tow. But that morning, the fact that the Attorney-General himself had taken the trouble to be there moved me deeply; and how could I not be touched by all those who had waited patiently to greet me in person?

From the airport I travelled to the Hotel. This was to be my base for a few days while I fulfilled by obligations to the Young Turks and found my bearings. Kingstown was as beautiful as I remembered it, small, self-contained, the harbour bewitchingly tranquil. The streets bustled; there was energy to the compact capital city. After a week it was time to move to visit my aunt where I lived before.

I had been so busy taking in the sights, meeting people, appearing on the radio, that the thought of the place had almost slipped from my mind. Now, as the hour approached, I took a moment to compose myself. A slight apprehension about our first meeting remained, but I told myself to go with an open mind. If I could rid myself of the baggage we could begin again.

All my fears disappeared the moment we met. My aunt was genuinely pleased to see me, as were the children. They were proud of my achievement, they said, and I could see that they meant it, I was to make myself at home. None of the old feelings came between us, my stay there was extremely pleasant.

My aunt died in December 2014. When I last saw her a year earlier in SVG she had had a stroke, but her mind was surprisingly sharp. She recognized me without difficulty, we talked about our families, it was clear that the past had been buried although she probably didn't truly appreciate how miserable I had been during my initial spell there. She was ill, but she still had her faculties, and she reminded me of something I had forgotten. When I got my first pay packet from my laundrette job in England I had written her and sent her some money. She had appreciated this very much, she said, and I was very pleased to hear her say that about my small gesture of thanks.

So they welcomed me as a family member. There was no bitterness or suspicion, I was no longer the confused little girl. We didn't delve into the past, how much they knew about what I had been through I couldn't tell. They took me for the family member I was, and showed me the full extent of their hospitality. I ate what they prepared; the young girl who had washed and ironed with a bitter frown was now a welcome guest.

Every returning Vincentian has a tale of a friend or family member eyeing up the clothes on their back, a favourite shoe, a hat or an expensive perfume. Some of these returnees get annoyed, some snort in frustration; they would give what they can afford, they don't need to be told that by those who treat them well. This was the only irritation. One of the daughters who was a constant companion approached me with that sly look that put me on my guard instantly. Could she have a particular dress, she asked, she would be truly grateful.

I could only chuckle to myself at her cheek. She didn't consider that it might have been a favourite dress, the price didn't come into it: she liked it, could she have it? I didn't let the demand spoil my relationship with my aunt's family.

Over the course of my holiday, like a child roused from a long illness, I would gaze in amazement at the beauty of the island. The lushness, the colours of the trees and flowers, the breath-taking landscape. Birds, butterflies, insects, I hardly noticed them in England, yet here they were, a natural part of the life of the island.

WITH YOU TONIGHT

The force of the sun surprised me, and closeness of the sea. The warmth of the people, also. No matter where I went Vincentians came to shake my hand, they took great pride in my work, they wanted to thank me in person for putting the island on the map. I remember sitting in a café one day and hearing an announcement on the radio: "Welcome home, DD".

The time I spent in SVG was just the fillip I needed after the struggles I had been through. People put aside what they were doing to make me feel welcome, everyone wanted a peek at this person whose songs boomed from their radio.

I did a show, the response of the audience was overwhelming. In the glitzy atmosphere of European arenas where I had performed thousands had turned out to show their appreciation, now my fellow Vincentians arrived in droves to let me know they appreciated my musical contribution. Many would have a long and dangerous journey home by minivan late in the evening, nodding off as the van negotiated the sharp corners of the leeward highway, others would hear the rasping sea on the windward roads. The grip of winter cold Europe seemed distant, preforming in the Caribbean, with the heat and the sweet perfume of the night air was a heady experience indeed.

Everywhere I went I was made to feel special. No one held it against me that I had been away for two decades, youngsters who recognized me only from the posters, radio, television and my songs flocked to celebrate my return. But the response when I first went back to Dickson, my village, was on an altogether different level.

I had expected a quick visit with a news crew attracting perhaps a dozen or so people curious to see what I looked like in the flesh, or family members proud to hug and greet me and say 'Welcome back'. It was anything but. Whenever I play the video the SVG news team made that day I'm still bowled over by the reception I received.

Shout 'murder', anywhere in SVG and within minutes you can guarantee a sizeable crowd. Oblivious to the possible danger, people will sprint in the direction of the holler, bubbling pots will be abandoned on a blazing fire, young or dry coconuts will remain unpeeled, children will scamper from their chores, students their times tables, beers will stand on shop counters warming with every passing hot minute, dominoes games left in the balance. The reception waiting for me when I returned to my home village was on par with a woman finding another woman in her home and bawling 'murder'. It has to be one of the most thrilling things in my life. The SVG news crew captured the entire event and presented it to me on a VHS video. They probably don't fully appreciate the significance of those 20 minutes of news tapes but I thank them from the bottom of my heart.

As I have said, I had expected a short visit, a few diffident 'hellos' and some quiet reminiscences with those closely connected with the family. I also expected a pose at the places where I picked fruits as a child, a recreation of the route I took on my way to and from school, the landmarks that dwell in our minds for some reason we will never know, the midwife who delivered me I expected to remind me of the fact, and perhaps a half-remembered relative with some embarrassing tale to entertain my travelling companions from England. The throng that descended surprised everyone and the film of that day is something to behold.

A reporter from SVG News is in the news coverage. A friend, my 'partner' at the time features too; I wonder what he made of the general hullaballoo? For my homecoming was like a festival. Everyone wanted to shake my hand to tug my dress, to tell me some story they remembered or had heard. I listened, and laughed where the story was vaguely familiar. When the tale was one I couldn't recognize I stored it in my memory for later. The video shows several people dancing and me going from house to house in the village, shaking hands, trying to remember the places where I played as a child and the scenes of my little adventures. What a time!

It was like a carnival, a Rasta man commented; the villagers truly appreciated what I had done for them. How much could I remember of the village, the reporter asked? I was able to point out where I used to play as a girl, and the position of an avocado tree. It was curious how, despite the years, the memories came flooding back. Neighbours helped to fill in the gaps in my remembrances, I was grateful that they had taken such an intense interest in my life. The noisy reception I got an hour earlier should have told me what to expect. But not even in my wildest dream would I have believed this many people were interested in me. I visited the house in which I grew up, even now I wonder how such a small place could have sheltered so many of us without constant argument.

But it did, and it made us the people we are today; a tight and loving family, one that looks back on our upbringing without an ounce of regret. I met my sister and her family again, it was a second emotional reunion. Some of my father's relatives presented themselves, other family members prayed that I wouldn't forget them. Of the people I could identify right away were close family members. I left the village feeling elated, knowing that, from humble beginnings we can still dream and with a little luck, some of us can not only play on the world stage but strut on it.

After Dickson I returned to Kingstown, alternating between Sunset Shores. Being based near the capital made it easier to get around, Kingstown was the heartbeat of the island, the home of the media and press. I was invited as a guest for the day and had a wonderful time. I was welcomed as an important guest and given my own chalet. It is a magical island and I felt honoured to have been invited.

I had never been to the awe-inspiring islets so when he heard this, he decided that he had to put things right. 'Well,' he said, 'you're here now, welcome home. I'm going to give you something to remember.'

He chartered a boat and told me I could take my friends and relatives to any of the Grenadines islands I fancied. I chose Bequia, probably because it was the closest to mainland St Vincent or someone might well have recommended it, I can't remember the reason for my choice. Whichever it was, I'm glad that this was the island I settled on. It was an enchanting place, and still is. It lived up to all expectations, in fact it easily surpassed them for charm and natural beauty.

As we pulled into port I gasped in wonder at the magnificence of the place. Such splendour sends us back to a childhood state and it brought out the child in me. It reminded me that beauty is one of the qualities that give meaning to our lives. Even today I love the slow ferry journey between St Vincent and Bequia. Standing on the deck I once saw a whale heading for Bequia as we were sailing in the opposite direction. It was a magnificent spectacle. Dolphins are visible in the clear blue waters, flying fish and a host of others I can't identify, each journey to or from Bequia is like a childhood adventure.

We devoured the local food we had cooked that long hot day, we drank, swam in the warm blue-green sea, we raced on the hot white sand; it was the kind of day that lingers forever in the memory. In the company of friends, it was an extremely satisfying experience on a small quiet island that allows you to create your own enjoyment. As we left in the early evening, tired, full, deliriously happy, on the journey back to mainland St Vincent on the ferry, I made up my mind that should I return to the Caribbean, Bequia would be my home, God's willing.

I spent the rest of the holiday sight-seeing and catching up with relatives and friends, and making new ones. At the back of my mind was the feeling that two weeks was too short; but a fortnight I had booked, so a fortnight it was. Yet there were so many people to meet, too little time to visit all the historic landmarks.

My contacts wanted to know where I had been, what I had seen, they were determined to ensure that I made up for all I had missed. One of the people I met hosted a radio show, and he hastily arranged a show at a club. She was outspoken and opinionated and his radio show had thousands of listeners. The show's on me, she said, with typical generosity 'in recognition of the unofficial ambassadorial work you've done for the country'; neither us realised the consequences of this act of gratitude.

The club is situated yards from the glorious beach looking over the island. It is a perfect and romantic setting. When the international airport opens, it will surely become a favourite spot with tourists and returning nationals alike. The night she had booked me in at the club was beautiful, fragrant, the stuff of dreams. My holiday was nearing its end and I wanted to leave on a high note, in every way. I performed, and once more the reception was overwhelming. I had repaid the Young Turks for the invitation and now, to end my stay, I had put on a performance for the hundreds. These were a fitting set of memories to take back to England, I decided, as we drive back, my head still full of the laughter and gaiety of the evening, the waves creeping silently to the nearby shores.

The show finished quite late. It had been a brilliant event, so many people to talk to and dozens to swap stories with. If I had forgotten how wonderfully charming a Caribbean night could be, this one gave me a gentle reminder to take with me back to England. Spread the news, it seemed to say if nights could talk, let those in England who have forgotten their home know what is waiting for them, a simple plane ride away. But we were all tired and ready for our bed, driver as well as passengers. The laughter and talk soon gave way to yawning and droopy eyes, all we wanted was to get home as quickly as possible.

The journey to the hotel at that late hour was probably no more than twenty minutes. Unfortunately - we realized later - the driver fell asleep at the wheel for an instant. And in that instant, it seemed that my life was over.

There had been no warning. Suddenly the van swerved viciously and we knew that something was wrong. I'm not sure exactly where this occurred. As I glanced quickly out the window, I could make out a sheer half mile drop to our left. In the darkness disaster beckoned, I was sure that the end was nigh. The terror! My heart clacked loudly and horribly; I was petrified. After such a brilliant time in my homeland I was going to end my days in a crumpled vehicle at the bottom of a cliff in the early hours of the morning!

Each terrifying second seemed like an hour. There wasn't time to scream or anything. All I remember is that gut-wrenching feeling, that sense of events being out of your control. Why? Why? Why me? Why now? My mind clouded as I tried to make sense of what was happening. You hear of your life accelerating away at the speed of light at moments of crisis, a million images flashing before your eyes, and this was how I felt. Fortunately, one of the left wheels of the vehicle dropped into a drain and got stuck. The drain had trapped it and prevented it tumbling down to what would have been certain disaster. The drama was all over in such a short time I wondered what the other passengers made of it. We had had a lucky escape. I couldn't sleep that night and for weeks afterwards I had nightmares about that journey.

I had enjoyed my stay immensely but my other life in England was never far from my mind. I often wondered what my children were up to, I sometimes wished Mom was with me to share some of the fruits of my success. She had done so much for me, offering encouragement or looking after the children, she deserved a holiday too. But that was for another time.

But for now, it was time to prepare myself for the journey back to England; the long flight, the shift from hot to cold. Leaving SVG was extremely difficult on that visit as it is on every other. My sister was there to see me off, as were the Attorney-General and people close to me. I thanked them for their hospitality, I was truly grateful for the opportunity they had given me. It had taken the invitation to open my eyes, to remind me that there was another world out there where people cared for me, people I cared for deeply too.

Even as we chatted and I thanked them profusely, and later, as the aircraft prepared for the trip to Barbados, I swore that never again would I stay away from my country for more than a year. I could see what my friends and relatives had been talking about, I was the one who had been missing out. England has been good to us, it is our home, but we are like the woman in my major hit, we have two loves and we have to make a choice.

And I have stuck to the promise I made before boarding and while I strapped in for the flight to Barbados. Whenever I do a show in St Lucia or some other nearby country I made sure I pop home, even if it's for a couple of days.

My only regret was that my children and my mother hadn't been able to share the holiday. My children would have to wait until their major exams were out of the way before their first visit to the Caribbean. It's a place they came to love dearly, although for my daughter, at first anyway, the mosquitoes made her life hell and she would have to wear socks to keep them away from her juicy 'British' blood.

CHAPTER FOURTEEN

Litigation

WHEN I RETURNED TO ENGLAND from the trip to St Vincent and the Grenadines, it seemed only natural to take stock of my life. The sunshine days had been filled with activity, people wanting to see me, enquiring about relatives or friends, or doing radio interviews, but the more I tried to satisfy this new curious public the clearer it dawned on me that I had to get my life in order. There were too many loose ends and I had to put to bed as many of the uncertainties as I could.

The people of SVG had seen me as an international artist, the British public thought of me similarly, and the Europeans had shown their approval by turning out in their thousands at my shows. None of these three groups knew the details of my situation, of course, and I doubt whether they would have been interested. And rightly so. I had scored two major international hits, they loved the records, they enjoyed my live performances, everyone was content. What I had been through, the nights of torture with my husband, the self-doubt I had endured with the producer, weren't their concern.

As I've tried to show, there had been many dark nights: the pressure of husband's descent into instability and finally full-blown madness, the struggle to complete the album under the unsympathetic eye of a producer who couldn't be bothered to try to see things from my perspective, it had been a real trial but I had come out on the right side. No one could accuse me of being a shirker, but now it was time to consider my long-term future and that of my children. Which one of us wouldn't seek justice? Who would entrust their future to luck and chance?

There was a trip to Dubai to fulfil, and appearances in Africa and the Caribbean in the pipeline, but royalties from my recordings were still laughable. There I was, an artist with sales topping a million and still financially insecure! The public believed that I was sleeping in a bed of crisp, freshly-wrought pound notes when, in reality, I spent my nights worrying about not being able to pay the mortgage somewhere down the line. But I am a positive person, I always believe in looking forward and that was my state of mind when I sat down to take stock after the definite fortnight in SVG.

During my travels overseas or within the UK to gain what I could from personal appearances, Mom would step in to look after the children. Go, she would urge, my children will be fine with me, get out there and please your public. Entertain those who buy your records, videos and CDs, give them what they want. I appreciated her help; I couldn't have achieved a fraction of what I have without her backing. But, welcome as they were, my earnings from town hall guest appearances, night club bookings, and so on, couldn't provide enough to run a household, put my daughter through university, and look after her brother's education. I could see the day approaching when the mortgage and the gas and electricity would be a problem again and I had no intention of allowing that to happen.

I had enrolled my son in a boarding school and now that I was at home full time it made sense to have him back. School fees took a fair proportion of my income, the extras for clothes, sporting equipment, trips and other sundries crept up on my shrinking purse. Any savings I could possibly make I had to seriously consider. So I contacted the boarding school and informed them of my decision. I couldn't afford the fees, I was candid with the staff, I was thinking of transferring my son to mainstream education. My son had cursed me when I first placed him in this school in Reading, 20 miles from his friends and family, but now that he was settled, I got the impression that he would have been quite happy to remain there until university.

And the school was desperate to hang on to him. He was an exceptional student, they argued, it was coming up to a critical time in his education, this wasn't the moment to transfer a pupil to another institution. But I was adamant. We hadn't had anything approaching a 'normal' family life for several years,

home was the best place for him in every respect now.

But the school was equally determined and extremely persuasive. The teachers had planned for him to continue his senior education at Stowe, a private school; there were scholarships available, they felt confident that he would get one. 'Might' and 'would' are fine words but no guarantee, I pointed out during one of our many discussions. Besides, scholarships generally came with strings attached, you had to do this, you can't do that. When the boarding school saw that I wouldn't budge from my position, they agreed to prepare him for the examination.

Buckinghamshire is, I believe, one of three counties in England which still persists with this test. Pupils sit papers in English, Maths and Verbal Reasoning, designed, say the authorities, to select those with academic potential, irrespective of social background. In reality, some pupils have a knack at answering these multiple choice questions; others don't, even with private lessons or long term coaching. The top scorers from each primary school have the choice of grammar or high school, the remaining students usually opt for the closest secondary school, unless the school's academic reputation is dire, when they seek a better alternative.

Which school did I want my son to attend? He had an unorthodox way of learning languages, his boarding school said, the teachers had never seen a student like him. I chose the royal school. It is widely regarded as the top boys' school, why settle for the second best? When he duly passed the stiff exam that autumn, the local authority awarded him a place at the best school possible. Naturally, I appealed. I put to the Appeals panel the evidence of his academic work at the boarding school and their recommendation. Soon after, thankfully, he was placed at the royal school.

I was happy, for not only was he back at home with me, but he would attend a school with very high academic standards and one that was a bus stop away.

After the success of my records and the appearances on Top of the Pops, several major record companies approached me. They were in the business of promoting the best artists, it was only fair to test the waters, they suggested, to see if and how we might be able to move forward together. I had captured the public's imagination, the video had added an extra dimension to my work, these companies wanted to see if we might be able to come to some mutually satisfactory recording arrangement.

Their representatives took me out to lunch and dinner, laid on the champagne, discussed possible scenarios. I got to know the big hitters and they wanted to know about me, about my musical tastes and influences, about my future direction in the music industry. I was a superstar in their eyes, one with more than a million sales behind me, I deserved the best. I was young, they reminded me, I had excellent dress sense, I projected myself well, spoke eloquently but without pretence or affectations, they could see great possibilities if we could set up as a team. There was even talk of one of the labels to produce me. I could sense the excitement in the voices of these executives with marketing expertise and millions at their disposal, the best studios, engineers, and musicians at their beck and call.

But first there was the issue of contracts. One major company was the forerunner, I won't say which, but they had a stable of several major reggae artists and saw me as a welcome addition to their Caribbean output. Most of their signings were male, perhaps they were looking to counterbalance this. They were aware that I was contracted to a label, they remarked, but felt that there was a possibility of coming to some mutually beneficial arrangement. When I showed them my contract, the executive examined it carefully, and I remember him covering his mouth in horror, like someone who had received a sudden shock, or who had unintentionally let out a swear word in public. Then he covered his eyes, as if he couldn't believe what he had read.

'What have you done?' he asked after a minute or so. 'Did you sign this contract?' I tried to explain how this came about. I used to sing with a band, I indicated, the album from which the hit singles had been drawn, was my introduction to recording. Yes, I had put my name to the agreement, I answered. I was a novice to the industry, I had taken on the project out of a sense of duty to my composer not realizing the full implications, and I had signed the contract in good faith, assuming that a fellow West Indian would have my best interest at heart. The representative listened to my woeful tale still in a state of disbelief. Did I realize that the contract could bind me to the record company for life, he continued? Was I aware that I had practically signed my life away?

I thought back to the days of recording the album, to the evenings and nights spent promoting it, to the attitude of the record producer and his wife to the singer who, even as we sat there, were sitting pretty on a small fortune. And all thanks to me! I was 'their artist', they took great pleasure in reminding me, they had supposedly spent 'huge sums' on me so I had to do as they directed. The thousands of pounds coming their way seemed to have gone to their heads, the more records they sold the more monstrous they seemed to grow.

I remember being in the middle of an interview when I got a call from the wife wanting me to attend another engagement. 'Where are you?' she hollered, like a mother wondering why her teenage daughter was late from school. 'We're spending a fortune on you, where the hell are you?' And, minutes later, guess who was running to catch a taxi to London, shoes in hand, like a fool, or a puppet being strung from a distance?

Everything they required in terms of promotion I had fulfilled. For the Jamaican Independence celebration that year at the town hall I had spent hundreds on clothes, shoes and my hair to project the image the record label demanded. I did a stint at a big carnival event, anywhere they directed I went, wearing my best smile, singing my heart out. Never mind the inconvenience. Ignore the aggravation behind the scenes. The record was selling by the cartload, a singer can get away with many things but letting down the public wasn't one of them.

I remembered as well that I was on the way to Germany on morning, had almost reached the airport when a call came through from the company. They wanted me to fly to Greece directly afterwards, the record was charting there, the signs were good, a spot of promotion would do the trick. I was so upset. I had planned to return home directly after the German concert, I hadn't made arrangements for the children. Mom lived 5 miles away, it wasn't fair on her to be racing between the two to take care of her grandchildren after a hard day at the factory.

Then there was what I saw as the producer's stubborn ignorance, his refusal to license the records to an American company. Such a huge market, Canada too, promotions, the power of the media in North America. Large Caribbean communities in Brooklyn, New York and Toronto, what a missed opportunity! I can still hear his gruff voice in my ears grumbling that they wanted to steal his artist and he would not allow that.

I couldn't see myself continuing with this label. I had recorded the album as promised, had found myself at the venues they suggested to plug the songs, paid the fares to get there, bought the outfits befitting a major artist without a single contribution from them. The rewards were landing in their basket, they were busy now, the wife had grown so self-important she deserved a serious slap to fix her face. I had signed an agreement, they said when I pointed out the one-sidedness of the document, I had no choice but to honour it. 'Slavery is over,' I had to remind them, 'I want out.'

Determined to settle a few scores and to get what I was owed I went to see a firm of solicitors in London. I carefully explained the position I found myself in and showed them the contract I had signed several months into recording the album. They were professional, they were able to see things from my point of view unlike the previous firm I had asked to go over the document. Taking time over the details, the contract was examined with a thoroughness I couldn't help but admire. At the end of their examination the firm explained that litigation was very costly and outlined the options open to me. They were at pains to point out that the law moved at a slow tempo, a pace that could be frustrating to all involved, and urged me to be patient. I understood, I told them, and appreciated their guidance. All I wanted was justice, I couldn't honour for much longer a contract that was so blatantly unjust.

The solicitors then wrote to the record company demanding copies of sales and royalties which they duly passed on to me. When they saw the phenomenal sales the producer had declared they wrote to demand 'a bigger bite of the cherry' as I instructed them. My music had scored in countries far and wide, total sales exceeded any figure I had supposed. I had signed a contract, the record producer responded to the solicitors with typical arrogance: I had put my name to the contract without coercion, I had no choice but to honour it. 'No way,' I was adamant with my solicitors, 'over my dead body.'

The law has a slow rhythm, the solicitors had warned me, but you don't fully realize the true significance of this statement until you're actually locked in a case. I suppose I'm one of those people who, believing that right is on their side, feel that they will get the opportunity to put their case sooner rather than later. That didn't happen. It took a full year for the case to get to the High Court. A long frustrating year when all sorts of thoughts churned away in my mind, a year I would rather forget.

There was an engagement to fulfil in Dubai, and several guest appearances throughout Britain, but in between these events I was at home twiddling my thumb. Sought out and made to feel important one day, people flocking to catch a glimpse of the woman who had brought them two love songs they dearly cherished, the next I would find myself depressed and miserable. There was so much more music in me, songs I knew my fans would love, but, with the legal battle waiting to be played out, my creative energies were being stifled. It was like being slowly strangled, the air trickling from the lungs, bubble by slow bubble. Singing was now my future, but that future looked as bleak now as during the period with my husband.

During this time, of course, all the record companies who had been interested in me began to look elsewhere. There were always new singers springing up, starlets and songsters seeking fame and glory, no company is going to touch with a bargepole an artist with contractual problems, it's just not worth their while. Strike while the iron is hot, is their motto, and with good reason. By the time contracts have been sorted, the public might have moved on to some other singer, record companies are in the business of selling here and now, they have to keep in tune with the buying public, some other singer would have plugged the gap I had left.

So after the initial excitement at the prospect of working with another label, of the thought of a more professional and understanding producer, as the months dragged on, I wasn't recording, I was idle in every sense of the word. I had given up my job at the medical company, I was stuck at home watching my plants grow and wither with the change of seasons. I was eating into the pittance I had received from the record company, and the payments for my live shows were going the same way. This couldn't go on. I couldn't wish away the mortgage, I had to find myself a job to pay for electricity, gas, house and car insurance, and the seemingly never-ending demands that drop through the letterbox.

I had come to England at 15 without qualifications, had done several months of a secretarial course at college, but the reality was that I had very little to fall back on. Nowadays parents are at pains to drill into their children the importance of education, A levels are the bare minimum for a good job, we tell them they need to aim for a degree to open up the world. Back in the 60s, 70s and 80s, fresh from the West Indies, our parents took the first job that came along and most of us were inclined to do the same. Employment gave us the security we didn't have in the Caribbean, parents seldom thought in terms of careers and this rubbed off on us. My singing had led me into a world of promise, had fulfilled dreams I had not dared to dream, but my recording career depended on too many undependable people: I had to find a secure job to look after the monthly outgoings.

There was no way I could go back to factory work, I had moved on in too many ways; I wanted something more challenging and rewarding, the days of packing and boxing were long gone. Try something new, my mind said to me, even though you don't have formal qualifications you have experience and you're not short of common-sense. Hard work didn't faze me, I was prepared to do what it took to get my children the education I had never had so that they could set themselves up as so many of our Caribbean youngsters are doing.

One day, during this period of considering my future, I saw a position being advertised at a district council. The job was for basic administration, contact with the public, that sort of thing. It might have specified experience, qualifications also, I don't remember. It sounded like a role I could fill, so I completed the application form, more in hope than anything else.

Lo and behold they invited me for an interview! Me, who didn't have formal qualifications and who had never dealt with the public outside singing was in the running for a fulltime post. It was an eerie experience because I had never had a proper interview for a job.

I didn't know the sorts of questions they asked, I hadn't prepared any answers as any youngster today would be encouraged to do. I would trust my instincts, I decided, when all else fail, rely on that judgement that's built into all of us. Show them who you are, the true you, if there is such a thing.

It's difficult to say if it was a demanding interview because I haven't been to many. When I left the room, I didn't know whether I had done well or badly. I had given it a go, that was the main thing, but, by the time I got home someone was on the phone with news of the outcome: I had gotten the job. The interviewer had no way of knowing how happy I was to have landed something to bring in some steady income. It was an administrative post but to me it was like a small win on the lottery.

Eventually, after a year that seemed like 10, my case came before the High Court. I had waited for so long when the day came it was an enormous relief. The High Court is every bit as daunting as its name suggests. It is a historic building, and I stepped into its famous court with a mixture of anticipation and trepidation, praying that it would find in our favour. I hadn't seen the producer and his overbearing wife for some time and now, face to face, I had nothing but contempt for them as we took our places for the hearing.

The case was put before the judge, dressed in all his finery. The details of the record sales and royalties were before him, he scrutinized them then turned to me. Had I received an advance from the company? Did they pay for my costumes to appear at these promotional events? No was the answer to them both I answered firmly and simply. The judge asked a few more questions and took submissions from both parties. Then we listened in silence as he gave his verdict.

The contract was null and void, he pronounced, in a stern voice. My heart rose with joy at the sound of these words. 'They didn't make contracts like that anymore,' he added, and I thought back to the first firm of solicitors who had pronounced it fair. 'Fifty percent of the album belongs to her,' he continued, 'but the label is allowed to "exploit" the recordings.' They could continue to benefit from our collaboration, provided I received a fair share. How did the producer react to the judgement? I was to find out in due course.

Things were kicking off in South Africa, the video I had made had made its way there, the interest was something to behold. A reasonable man would have grabbed the opportunity to make a handsome profit for us both but this man wasn't reasonable by any definition of the word. He wanted it all.

They had made a bundle from all my hits, instead of looking forward to a second lucrative album, they seemed determined to shake every ripe mango from the branch then chop the branch from the tree. Many believed that my composer, who had written the colossal hit, was a millionaire! He had to be! After all, hadn't the song topped the British charts? Hadn't it taken off in Europe too, and countries as far as Australia?

But he hadn't cleaned up, as people thought, and still think now. I gather that he wasn't happy and, if my contract was anything to go by, I suspect that his was equally one-sided.

The royalties were to be paid to me on the first of July 1990, the judge had directed. I was due exactly half, the judge had made it clear, not the pittance I had received. As the day approached, I had mixed feelings. A fair share of the profits would be welcome, naturally, but I knew how the producer operated, I couldn't see him going down the path the judge had directed without a fight.

On the 30th June I had my answer. The label had filed for bankruptcy, my solicitors informed me.

How did I take the news? It felt as though I had been kicked in the stomach. I was stunned, angry, hurt, bitter. Life seemed so unjust, I felt like crying with frustration and rage. I felt powerless, the way you do when you are wrongly accused and you have no way of getting back at your accusers. That this man could make a mockery of me and the law in one day made this one of the lowest points of my life.

But I wasn't low for long. Money has its purpose but life is much more than crisp pounds or well-thumbed dollars. 'I never had it,' I consoled myself when the news had properly sunk in, 'I will never miss it.'

I gathered that the producer had tried to sign an English band in an effort to get rid of some of his assets. I was also told that he had bought a hotel in the Caribbean. I had no proof and, to be honest, I don't really give a damn now. That chapter of my life is closed. I have moved on and I don't spend my nights wondering what has become of him.

CHAPTER FIFTEEN

South Africa

SOUTH AFRICA IS WITHOUT QUESTION where my greatest fan base is situated. I go there regularly to perform and the reception I receive has never been less than tremendous. It's a country I love dearly; the people are like no other in their appreciation and generosity.

But I'm aware that my visits there have been shrouded in controversy, especially the first one, in 1989. Even now some of my friends are unhappy that I went. It was a mistake, they argue. There was a general boycott and my action amounted to support for the despicable apartheid regime. My answer now is similar to what it is then: I didn't jump at the first opportunity to go there, I went after much soul-searching and reflection. And I undertook the trip in response to the pleas from the black community there. They wanted me desperately, I was told, my refusal would have meant disappointing a whole heap of people.

But there was another strand to my decision, some might call it selfish but it was what it was. A singer's life is a precarious, I tried to get over to those who tried to dissuade me, the record had taken off there in a way that surpassed all expectations, the people were clamouring for me, so I took the decision to appear before them in that spirit. When opportunities arise, we have to examine them carefully, and that's what I felt I did.

The invitation to tour came out of the blue. Someone had taken the album to South Africa and soon after there was a call and one message after the other. 'We need you to come to South Africa,' a representative of a famous record company pleaded. 'The people are going crazy for you.' A letter I have in my possession,

gives an idea of the mood there. It is dated September 1989. 'When will you come and visit my country,' she wrote, 'hope soon.

'No way,' was my initial reply to the record executive, for I had no intention of going when the initial request came. The boycott wasn't the first thought that came to mind, it was the despicable way black people were treated in that country. Television brought the grim pictures, the behaviour of those in power was as shocking as it was incomprehensible. There was no chance of me allowing myself to be put in a position where I might be humiliated because of my colour.

It's not like that, I was told by the potential sponsors when I expressed my misgivings, hotels weren't segregated, my fears about being restricted to where I went, slept, or who I came into contact with were ill-founded. 'Come and see for yourself,' I was told things had changed and were improving for blacks each day.

Coming unexpectedly as it did and at a time when I didn't know what the future held, I came round to the view that I should at least weigh up the issues before making up my mind. When the company pointed out that ordinary people would be disappointed if I didn't show up, that they were at fever pitch after seeing copies of the video, I tried to come to the best solution for those who wanted to see me in person, for the company, and, yes, for myself.

How would I be treated if I decided to go? Now that I had begun to explore the options open to me, a set of questions suggested themselves. Who exactly were my fans? Were they white South Africans or black? How many people were there in reality, hundreds, thousands? Would there be separate venues, would black people be barred from the arenas they had booked for my appearances?

I wrestled with these questions daily as I considered the invitation and its possible ramifications. The record company was going out of its way to show me all the positives that might come from even a brief appearance, I decided to seek advice outside my family and the friends who expressed their reservations.

A certain musician's union, of which I wasn't a member, recommended that I observed the boycott. Any member who performed in South Africa faced a heavy fine or expulsion from the union, its policy was crystal clear. The boycott had been in place for 30 years and it wasn't interested in whether or not members played to mixed or segregated audiences. Equity, the actors establishment, of which I was a member, had a slightly different take on the matter. I could go, it advised, but for promotion only, not to perform. I could make guest appearances, talk, do anything but sing. Miming was prohibited also, it stressed, should a member be tempted to flirt with the idea.

Equity's stance sounded like a reasonable compromise to me. The records were selling in enormous quantities, I would go and promote them, and see for myself if there might be opportunities for the future.

Yet even as I came to this position my conscience gave me sleepless nights. I had visions of appearing at venues where the black population was excluded or where the entrance fee was set artificially high so that only those with a healthy salary could afford it. I sought guarantees that I wasn't going to be relegated to some crummy hotel or be treated like a second-class citizen in any way, shape or form. If things had changed I would take the risk, go and plug my album, and prepare the groundwork for a possible future tour: I was prepared to see for myself if the developments the sponsors trumpeted were true, if the thousands they promised would materialize, or whether it was a crude ploy on the part of the record company to lure me there.

My sponsor had booked first class tickets and this initial contact I took as a sign of what was to come. Fortunately, it was in the positive direction. Fed a diet of stereotypes by the media, I had built up this image of blanket poverty and desolation and had lumped all the people of the country into two broad categories: rich whites with opulent lifestyles, blacks scratching a living. When I discovered that also stationed in first class were black businessmen and women, my heart lifted. I sensed that my decision to explore the country for myself might bear fruit after all.

The instant I arrived at Johannesburg Airport and was recognized people sprang from everywhere. I had never seen anything like it. For an instant I stood there wondering what had hit me. The commotion, the shouting and screaming and jostling, I had to pinch myself to make sure it wasn't a scene from some overhyped film. My visions had been of a low-key entrance to the country and perhaps dodging a scattering of protesters with placards. This greeting was like something from one of my wildest dreams. People poured in from everywhere, their eyes bright and inquisitive, their delight plain to see. The spontaneous reaction melted away all the doubts I had held. It felt like going on a blind date and discovering and old fancy. I was later informed that many simply abandoned their work for a moment and ran over to check that the person at immigration was truly me.

I was overwhelmed. I had expected nothing approaching this kind of reaction and the fact that so many wanted to greet me in person drove away the niggling doubts about going to South Africa. 'DD is here,' was the excited chorus as people craned their necks to get a glimpse, 'she's here, and she's here!'

How lucky I was! How lucky I am! What good fortune it was to be appreciated by so many people! And no matter how many times I return to South Africa, the feeling of humility and blessedness is never far away from my mind.

A press conference had been organized at the airport for me, and I expressed my sincere thanks for the warm welcome I had received. Keeping to myself the internal struggles I had faced, I was delighted to have finally made it, I said. After answering the myriad of questions and posing for photographs, I was driven to the hotel. I was shattered. A long night flight, the overwhelming reception, wondering what lay round the corner, I was drained. But I hardly noticed my physical state. So much had happened since I left London seven hours earlier it was easy to believe that I was creating my own fantasy.

As the sponsor had outlined, segregation was on the decline, a new enlightened country was being created. People mingled easily wherever I went or performed. If the tense atmosphere I had imagined descended on an event, it must have done so when I wasn't there, and each day I spent in the country deepened my love and amazement. I would be invited to do an interview and end up doing 10, often by phone.

For some reason I couldn't truly comprehend, the people took me to their hearts and I was left in no doubt that I had made the correct decision. My music was genuinely appreciated, I was no mere curiosity. In a country that has produced international artists such as Hugh Masakela, Miriam Makeba, Lucky Dube and Letta Mbulu among many others, to be welcomed and placed in the same category was truly gratifying. When you can perform for people accustomed to the haunting spiritual sounds of Ladysmith Black Mambazo you must have some true quality in you.

The physical beauty of the country matches that of the people. The day of my arrival taught me that. You hear of the wonders of South Africa and it's no exaggeration. The landscape simply knocks you out. Often, I stood wide-eyed and with my hand covering my mouth at the vista before me. During the two days I spent in Johannesburg, I felt small and in awe everywhere I went. Having grown up on a small island, the vast distances and grandeur of the place gave new meaning to the word magnificent. I stayed in this city for a couple of days and was presented with a quadruple award. The desire to see me, to see the person behind the voice never waned. I flew in a helicopter that monitored the traffic, the 'Eye in the Sky', and did a live interview; it was a wonderful introduction to a country I would fall in love with.

One of the most memorable events on this first visit was as a guest of honour at a luncheon, one of the most glamorous and prestigious events in South Africa. It was similar to the showbiz Water Rats. There were singers, magicians, dancers, entertainers of every kind, it was a truly grand occasion. The audience reflected everything the sponsors had promised, a mixed crowd, people of all races mingling just as they did in London. The arena was a splendid edifice, the atmosphere a reflection of the cream of the artistic talent of the country.

As one of the special guests, one of my tasks was to present an achievement award to a black lady, a former star. She is disabled now, and I could imagine her in all her glory thrilling theatregoers with the sureness of her voice and the exuberance of her dancing. Even with this brief biography I knew I couldn't simply thrust the award in her hand and offer congratulations. But I didn't have much experience of speaking in public. It is one thing to sing for a living, quite another to rely on your own words. How would I sound? How would I be received?

As the time approached, I began to wonder what I could say that wouldn't sound banal. In the end I decided to speak from the heart. At times like this I simply trust myself. I say things simply and honestly and that's what I did that evening.

'It was an honour, a privilege,' I said, 'for what more can one say when confronted with an artist who has served with distinction?' I could but imagine the impact she had made in the world-famous musical, the eyes of someone in the audience trained on her, oblivious to the rest of the cast, basking in the inner confidence on display. 'I hope that one day I could become someone of your stature,' I finished by saying, and I meant every word. There was an ovation that lasted for nearly five minutes and I sat down feeling meek and humble: God was on my side, I said to myself.

Cape Town was next on the agenda for an appearance at a shopping complex with a live radio link-up. On the drive, as we neared the complex, we noticed a sea of people all dressed up, all feverish with excitement. Where were they off to, I wondered? As the crowd swelled with people running from all directions, it was clear that there was some big event taking place in the neighbourhood. Someone famous had to be in town, there could be no other explanation. 'What's happening, I asked, what's going on?' As we got to the arena it hit me that we were all heading for the same destination.

My heart swelled. Imagine that, thousands of people all racing to catch a glimpse of me who, a few days earlier, had been torn between accepting the invitation and remaining at home wondering what the future held!

I appeared at the venue, greeted the crowd, accepted their applause, but, despite their requests, I didn't sing. They were desperate for me to but I explained the position and they accepted that. I did a live interview, answered their questions, and received their gifts. One man brought me a cow, there were offers of gold and clothing. To show my appreciation I reciprocated by lobbing some records and photographs into the crowd. Big mistake. Big big mistake. The moment I tossed them into the air the audience surged forward towards the radio set-up. The arrangement had thoughtfully placed the disabled and wheelchair users closest to the stage and now, as the feverish crowd heaved forward in the scramble for the souvenirs we feared for the worst. At that stage the blinds came hastily down. 'We can't continue,' the sponsor had a look of horror on his face. 'It's too dangerous.'

But still the fans kept chanting my name towards the end of the chorus. Thankfully, after the blinds went down, people remained where they were and the crush that had us covering our eyes and praying was averted. In the excitement and confusion, a tow truck had to get us out and drive us away.

The shopping centre management was very apologetic. Such a close shave! They thought I was going to sue them. 'What for?' I asked, not quite sure why they thought this. 'We didn't expect this many people,' they said, 'so we didn't plan for this. We've never seen anything like this. We had Lucky Dube here last week and nothing like this happened.' If that wasn't a compliment then nothing ever will be. At the time Lucky Dube was one of South Africa's biggest stars with a huge following not only on the continent but also in the Caribbean. Unfortunately, and sometimes it's hard to understand, he was shot dead in October 2007 in what was believed to be a carjacking.

This reception was a brilliant introduction to South Africa. The crowds, the push to see the singer who had brought them billboard hits. Many believed I was actually South African! On a subsequent tour one man would thank me for the help my songs gave him in 'breaking down his girlfriend'. Another said to me that the word among his friends was, 'DD is coming to South Africa, and we'll be making babies.' For several days after the reception at Newlands people were still talking about the event. My music helped them to get the girls, they admitted, without the slightest trace of irony. They didn't know how they could repay me for this.

I was a special guest of the sponsors on this first visit and they were determined to give me the star treatment. I was taken along the Garden route, the 200-mile stretch along the Western Cape that is a haven of forests and mountain streams, and home to beautiful flowers such as the pink protrea or sugarbush. Such a wonderful journey. I did the wine route, half an hour's drive from Cape Town, tasted the vintages, pretended I was a connoisseur. And then, finally, there was a trip to the Cape of Good Hope. Magnificent, awe-inspiring, stunning, words cannot do justice to this natural phenomenon.

Port Elizabeth was the next stop and George, names that are vague now revealed themselves in the form of beautiful African cities. The reception was just as enthusiastic. My visit was appreciated by those who had bought the records and videos. At times it was hard to believe that the album that had caused me so much pain and heartache, that I had journeyed to complete on cold and rainy Sundays, had reached so many. In the end, I suppose, none of that mattered. What the public heard, they loved. Sentimental, slow, lovey-

dovey, each song telling a tale in the space of three or so minutes, the songs touched the listeners. What more can a singer ask?

Namibia and Swaziland were part of that packed first trip also. They were independent countries and although it wasn't part of the agreement, I performed a hastily arranged show in the first and two in the second. In Namibia, this took place in a massive stadium in front of a mixed audience. Rehearsal was minimal, I had only met the musicians a few hours earlier, yet we managed to put on a show that thrilled the thousands of fans who turned up. And it was a similar situation in Swaziland. I appeared at the Royal Swazi Sun Hotel and in a nightclub. Once more the audiences were thrilled that I had made the effort, they thanked me profusely for visiting their beautiful country.

As the time to leave drew near I did a video shoot, giving me a further taste of the most exotic locations imaginable. In total I spent a truly wonderful 10 days in South Africa. Coming from a tiny Caribbean island of 150 square miles, the enormous distances seemed surreal. The vastness of the country took a while to get used to, but not the people. The welcome I received everywhere I went strengthened my belief that I had made the correct choice.

The first visit took place in 1989. Three years later I was invited back by the record company I had signed up with. The plan now was to record an album there with an old friend. A musician responsible for my first set of recordings, he was the consummate all-rounder and had laid down the tracks, I was to voice. Local musicians were brought in to add horns or keyboards and it was a pleasure to work with true professionals. After adding their contribution to a backing track they were never satisfied. 'Was that all right?' they would ask with genuine concern in their voices. 'Do you want me to do it one more time?' To see and hear players of this calibre at work was to acknowledge the heights that music can reach.

Then the album I recorded in South Africa was born. It took a mere four days to complete. Not because we rushed – the finished product is testimony to the quality of the compilation – but because we were able to give our full attention to the task in hand. There were no long trips or train rides; I made the short journey from the hotel to the recording studio in a taxi and spent the day voicing the tracks. When the producer was happy we went out to dinner, had a lavish meal, after which I returned to the hotel to rest.

The following day, the same; this was a true collaboration. I could make suggestions without feeling they would be dismissed out of hand, Lindell knew exactly the sound he was after and let me into the secret. It was a mature, professional and wonderful experience and I consider this to be one of my best albums.

To me the production oozed goodness. I had taken my time over the main and background vocals and I think it shows. There was no rushing to London to record and hurrying back late to catch a few hours before going to my day job. For the first time I was recording as a true artist; it was a wonderful way to work.

On my first trip to South Africa I didn't go to Soweto and I was determined to make up for the omission. The invitation duly came and I accepted without a moment's hesitation. When I mentioned to the producer that I was going there he was sceptical. He was a fellow West Indian and I found this curious. Perhaps he believed the horror stories. On the other hand he might not have realized the significance of our making a public visit. Whatever his reason, he was entitled to his opinion. You can't force people to do what they find uncomfortable or try to jolt them out of their indifference. I had no doubts though, for what would the people of Soweto think if I didn't appear there? 'You can stay in your hotel room,' I said to the producer, 'I'm going.'

And I had a day I couldn't fault. Unbelievable! It was, a day like no other. We hear so many things second-hand, we get so used to the stereotypes that we conjure up in our minds one vast lumpy space. We forget the individuality of the people who live there, we ignore that enterprise and resourcefulness of people who have to fashion a life for themselves without some of the modern conveniences we possess.

On the drive to the heart of the district we came across Mercedes, BMWs and a host of other luxury cars where I was expecting battered old jalopies. Perhaps the fault was mine. Perhaps I was the one who had forgotten the spirit of my own people and their drive and had expected nothing but vast townships and crippling poverty.

What I saw gave a lift to my heart. There were grand houses with enormous gardens well beyond the price range of people like myself. The trip included a visit to one of the best equipped hospitals, the schools and stadiums I was shown were equally impressive. I was taken to music venues, tasted the most delicious food. I met community leaders as well as the ordinary people who had bought my records and wanted to say how much they enjoyed them. In return I heard at close quarters the pulsating rhythms of the township and wider South Africa, rich and multi-layered with that thumping beat that makes you want to dance or shuffle your feet.

I left Soweto lamenting the power of the media. They feed the public a diet of gloom and despondency; they neglect to show the world the 'indestructible' spirit that exists there. There are townships, yes, there are poor people – lots of them – but what came over to me was their irrepressible attitude. People thrive there, they are ambitious, with the right combination of opportunity and luck, their prosperity will shock and delight.

Despite the hectic schedule they put in place for me when I performed there, it was always a privilege to return. The details of the 2004 tour will give some indication of what touring South Africa entails.

The following day I flew to Cape Town and checked into my hotel. On the Thursday there was an early live interview on a show at 8.30, then I had the day to myself. There was a sound check at noon the Friday and the show took place at 6pm. I caught the 20.05 plane back to London on the Saturday. A week in the country, but regretfully too little time to get around and meet the people and see the captivating sights.

Each visit to South Africa brings something new. In a country with such a strong musical heritage with its range of traditional and modern songs, I feel humble to have been accepted by its people on equal musical terms.

I remember distinctly the feeling that overcame me on my visit there in 2004 for the "South Africa Comes Alive Music Spectacular" at Carnival City's Big Top Arena on the East Rand. As I prepared myself for the trip, I remember distinctly praying that I might get an opportunity to meet the giants of that country, President Mandela, the legendary Miriam Makeba and Yvonne Chaka Chaka. Some dazzling surprise is always in store, each trip adds a layer of beauty to my life.

My last visit was in 2013. I was part of a show, in Cape Town. It was a true experience. The show took place at The Peoples Church in front of approximately 5,000 people. There was such a demand the promoters had to shift the furniture to accommodate the public.

I thank the people there for taking me to their hearts and hope that I have repaid their kindness and generosity with the force of my singing.

CHAPTER SIXTEEN

Mom

AFTER MY SISTER, MOM HAS had the greatest influence on my life. Her kindness and gentleness shone on me at a time when I was too young to appreciate such things. The weeks after she left for England, I was distraught.

Our reunion when I was 15 had come at just the right time, if not for her, then certainly for me. Admittedly we had to begin again after seven years apart, but I found a woman who was caring and protective. A causal but carefully chosen word here, a stern look or reminder there, she was the West Indian mother I was to become. Even so she allowed me the freedom to be a young woman, accepting that dancing, partying and late nights with friends are an essential part of growing up. And if she was disappointed when I fell pregnant she didn't show it. No ranting, no scowling, just a quiet pragmatism about where we were to live. She spoke her mind but didn't harbour malice. She was the person who encouraged me to give recording a try when others might have drawn up a list of all the possible pitfalls. Whatever I have achieved I owe in large part to her faith and encouragement.

But she was getting on. The job at the lighting company had taken a lot out of her and after caring for nine children, the sturdiest parent begins to feel the strain. When I travelled to perform, she would step in, even at the last minute, to look after my two children without a grumble. Like many people from the Caribbean she suffered from the dreaded duo, high blood pressure and diabetes. But she didn't let these conditions get in the way.

After she retired, she still tried to lead as active a life as possible. Sunday found her at church, during the week she attended the Multi-Racial Centre where she would meet some of her friends who had also stopped working, and she sometimes helped out looking after the elderly who needed help.

One Friday in May 1991, I popped in to see her at her home. We were in constant contact so there was nothing out of the ordinary in a quick visit. That day Mom was in what I can only describe as a euphoric state. It wasn't unusual to find her singing a hymn or humming some tune from her youth in the Caribbean, but the joyfulness and intense emotion struck me as odd. The hymns were mostly to do with 'going over to the other side', she was like a woman giving praises and thanking the Lord for her life on earth.

It was a bank holiday weekend with the traditional show, a mile or so from her home. My son and I were enjoying the fair when for some reason I couldn't fathom, he suggested that we should go and visit his granny. Some kind of premonition must have struck him, that's how I see it now on reflection. 'Let's go and visit granny,' he persisted, ignoring the attractions of the fair. I followed his suggestion, we went, and found her in a similar mood, singing, light-hearted, the way you feel when you finally settle a longstanding debt.

When we returned to my home, I was troubled. Something wasn't quite right but I couldn't put my finger on it. Was her mind starting to drift, was she in the early stages of dementia? 'The insurance is due,' Mom had reminded me several times and she had listed some of the other domestic tasks she wanted sorted. The urgency didn't make sense to me at the time, it seemed like one of those random statements we make every now and again for no apparent reason. 'Send for your sister,' she had said out of the blue, without explaining why, 'don't forget your sister.' I had left her home wondering what was going on in her mind.

The following Monday I found I couldn't sleep. I kept tossing and turning, my mind was racing through all kinds of strange thoughts, none of which I could latch onto with any conviction. Go downstairs and wait, a voice kept urging me, don't stay up here, wait downstairs. Was some important visitor about to arrive at that hour? And if so, who might it be? Less than five minutes had passed after obeying the silent instruction when the phone rang. It was my brother. He lived with Mom and he had found her sitting on the edge of the bed. She was dressed for church and had probably been resting before the short trip downstairs when her heart stopped.

What I did on hearing the news I can't remember exactly. She wasn't ill, she hadn't complained of any serious pain, how could she possibly slip away so quietly? After the shock time both raced and stood still, events merged into one another, I lost track of what was happening about me.

Hundreds of thoughts bombarded my brain as I sat down and tried to take in the magnitude of the news. I told the children, I'm sure; I did the practical things like contacting my siblings and close friends with the news. But all on automatic pilot. Mom, gone?

It didn't seem right, it seemed so unfair, as we all believe when one of our loved ones is called home. She was still young, was she ready in her mind? Had she prepared herself mentally to leave this world behind? Did she know she was ill, was she in pain? How would we cope without her?

We had never had a death in the family, it was quite a harrowing experience for us all.

Those who are unfortunate enough to have to lost a loved one will know that you get so wrapped up with the practical details that you forget to mourn for the departed. Not properly anyway. And that went for our family too. We sent for my older sister, my brother came over from Wales, the entire family rallied round. Each person helped in the preparations; we were determined to give Mom the kind of send-off she deserved.

When Mom was a young woman, she used to make ice cream to sell outside a famous progress hall, whenever a dance was taking place. This small enterprise brought much needed cash to help to raise us. Those who remembered her from those distant days came to pay their respects and hundreds more, locally, and from Reading, Oxford, London, Luton and Slough. As West Indians we have our faults, but support in a time of need or honouring those who have enriched our lives, can't be counted among them.

The turnout did justice to a hardworking mother, every memory I heard made me feel proud to be her daughter. That that many people had made the effort to pay their respects made the day for me. It was a fitting tribute to a popular and well-liked woman, undemonstrative and proud.

Having to deal with all the little details of a loss began to take its toll. On the eve of the funeral I felt really stressed. My throat became sore and tender, my entire body felt as though it was weighed down by this mighty force. I found it difficult to breathe, I felt rotten all over. I suppose I had bottled up my emotion, had spent so much time with the others on nitty gritty things that I hadn't properly sat down and taken stock of what Mom's departure was going to mean for us all. That night then, I could feel things getting on top of me and at the church the next day, there I was, my throat tight, as though an apple had got stuck in it, unable to sing a single hymn through the tears. 'Aren't you tired of crying?' my sister asked, 'haven't you cried enough?'

My sister was known in the family as the one who was hard and uncompromising, but even so I thought that was a bit much. How she could be so harsh? Couldn't she see the state I was in? I was crying because there I was, trying to force myself to join in the singing with my throat tender and painful, couldn't she appreciate that?

It was a cold May Thursday and there is nowhere more bitter and exposed than on the slope of the cemetery. But the mourners sang with all their vigour, as we wished Mom a safe passage to the other side. I remember that the hole was a bit too small, and that there had to be some hasty work to get things going smoothly. But, in the end, all went well and Mom had the rousing departure from this world that makes you proud to be a West Indian. And guess who lingered longest, crying her eyes out, and had to be pulled away? Yes, my older sister, the same sister who earlier had tried to maintain a hard front.

When the funeral was over and children and close relatives were all scattered again, I fell ill. I was weak, listless, I drifted from one day to the next. My illness was partly mental, partly physical, I expect. Mom had been a happy woman, hardworking, uncomplaining, she had wanted the best for her children and for her friends' children. She was there when you needed her. Now that she was gone and my father too, it felt like being cut loose in a canoe down a slow winding river. For to whom could I turn for advice? Who would be there to listen to my grumbling and tell me to get over it and get on with things?

My state of my mind began to affect my work. My sleep was on and off; I couldn't think straight. If someone had accused me of being a zombie then the accusation might have had some truth in it. To make it worse, word got back to me at work that there was a malicious rumour that I had asked the local newspaper, to cover the funeral. Two reporters had been spotted in the bushes, apparently, and the mischief-maker had seen fit to broadcast that their presence was something to do with me. What the person was trying to achieve I wasn't sure. What I was sure of was the effect the slander was having on me.

During my 23 years working there had always had its little cliques. Those who were lazy, who swanned about instead of earning their wages, were happy to point the finger at the rest of us who were determined to give a good service. People came to the office because they needed help or were vulnerable; the majority of the staff went out of their way to treat the customers with the dignity and respect they desired, but a small core of workers spent their time protecting the others in their little group instead of getting down to doing what they were paid for. And now, at a time when I was still grieving, they saw fit to wallow in their filthy gossip.

Of course, jealousy played a part in this. Customers to the office recognized me from my Top of the Tops or from my former band. They would strike up a conversation or some wanted autographs. This clearly rankled with those who would wish others to be at their level, and so things came to a head at the worst possible time for me. Just when I wanted some sympathy and understanding I was being accused of slacking and threatened with dismissal.

And then one day this man phoned about his mother's benefit. She hadn't received it, or hadn't received the correct amount, one of the two. 'You're killing my mother,' he sobbed, clearly distressed. On hearing this I broke down.

I was constantly in a state now. In a job that meant serving the public I simply wasn't in a frame of mind to do so effectively. I dithered, I was grumpy and moody, sometimes I was near tears. After my emotional reaction on the phone my supervisor arranged a meeting with the chief executive. She wanted me sacked, she had no qualms there. Instead of trying to understand my situation she saw it as a way of solving what she saw as a problem.

I stated the position as calmly and clearly as I could to the boss. Little cliques were undermining the good work of others, I informed him, the few bad apples were giving the place a bad name. My mother had recently died, I told him, and my work had suffered as a result. There were days when I didn't feel up to dealing with the public because of the cliques that existed.

The CE listened carefully and sympathetically. What would he decide, I wondered when I had finished my account? The state I was in, I truly didn't care. At that time, I couldn't be bothered about anything. Petty people had their little grievances and jealousies and I didn't want any part of it. A transfer to another team might be the best option, the CE concluded after thinking about it for a while, how did I feel about that?

I thanked him for listening and for the fresh start. I had spent 23 years there and, if nothing else, the experience toughened me up. When I first arrived, I was a softy, but I left knowing that I stood up for the people I worked with and for those clients who came to us in distress and left with their problem solved.

Even today I still think of my parents, especially my Mom. As I told the local papers at the time: 'She was a wonderful mother and very close to all her children and especially her grandchildren. She was very cheerful and always singing.'

Her friends recalled her singing all the way to Birmingham and back on one of their day trips. The community officer at that time praised her work with the clients at the centre for the elderly. 'She was an active member of the community and will be greatly missed,' he said. At the time she had 20 grandchildren and 15 great-grandchildren.

CHAPTER SEVENTEEN

Politics

I SUPPOSE THAT THIS IS a good place to mention my guest appearances for the two main political parties in St Vincent and the Grenadines, as some Vincentians have seen my singing at a rally as an 'issue'. Controversy is part of a singer's life, I suppose, and I certainly seem to have had my fair share.

My first involvement in this arena, if I could call it that, was for a political party. This party was founded in 1975. On my visit to perform a few years earlier, I had been welcomed by high-ranking government ministers including the Attorney-General; so when I was invited to perform, I regarded the invitation as a way of repaying their kindness and to acknowledge the rapturous welcome they had given me. I had helped to put SVG on the international map, the ministers had pointed out with undisguised pride, my role as an unofficial ambassador for the country was an important one.

That seemed reasonable enough, although I hadn't fully thought of myself in that way. West Indians in England frequently said similar things to me, but in a roundabout manner. What I achieved for myself, some made clear, was as nothing compared to what my accomplishments meant for them. When I appeared on television, I was their representative, they said, my success was theirs also, regardless of the Caribbean island of their birth. I didn't regard the hopes they pinned on me as a burden, I never allowed their comments to alter the way I performed or managed myself in public. I knew instinctively that wherever I went people would see me as a Caribbean woman (or a British one), and I like to believe that I conducted myself throughout my career with the necessary decorum and with suitable restraint.

Performer and ambassador, whatever life lobs at you, what choice do you have but to respond positively? Why dither and end up doing nothing when there is work to be done? That's how I see things. So when I was invited to appear at a rally, I didn't agonize over my decision. It was a resounding 'Yes'. For how could I turn down the opportunity to spend some time in my homeland and to perform for the fans who had received me so enthusiastically on my first visit? How could I decline the chance to say thank you in public to those officials who had taken time from their ministerial posts to greet me?

So I went to the rally, sang, renewed contacts, and made some new ones. I was again commended for my singing and reminded of my role as a representative for the Caribbean. Artists helped to boost the tourist industry, they emphasized, every little helped. If my appearance lifted the mood in the country, even temporarily, was that a bad thing? I always sang for the people, I was clear in my mind. The thought of townsfolk going home with smiles on their faces and with love in their hearts is what every singer strives for. If those who travelled back along the winding windward roads in the dark of evening felt the trip had been worth it then I was delighted. For those who were prepared to cope with the treacherous leeward hills on the way home at night, what could I say but thanks for the effort they had made?

One day in 2001, a call came through to me from a senior minister. After the usual greetings and preliminaries, he asked if I would like to come home.' I didn't know what he meant by this statement. 'Come home,' I asked, 'for what?' I could sense him searching for the right words.

He told me that the party was having a concert and wanted me to come home to heal the people.' A strong word, I remember thinking to myself, 'healing' sounded a daunting task.

There was an election looming, I knew, but I didn't want to be seen as throwing my weight behind a particular political party. Vincentians like myself who live abroad have our preferences, naturally, but we would be foolish to claim that we keep up to date with the affairs of the country to get a proper feel for what the parties stand for. I didn't wish to slight the minister who had phoned with the invitation but, equally, I wanted to make it clear that my appearance shouldn't be advertised in any way as support for any particular political philosophy. 'I'm coming to sing for the people of SVG,' I was at pains to stress, 'not for a party.' they accepted my point of view and a day was arranged for the performance.

A few weeks later off I flew with my producer/arranger, another long flight, the inevitable severe delay in Barbados. As a result we arrived at the Airport in SVG late at night, tired and stressed out. The Prime Minister himself, was there to greet us. He welcomed us with his customary warmth then we were driven to the hotel, not far away.

After an eight-hour flight from London, deep into the night before our heads hit the pillow, guess what? We had to be up at eight the following morning to prepare for the show! I suppose we hadn't thought it out properly, hadn't planned for delays, but the day was upon us so we had to deal with it. You have to, don't you? Yet it was tough. I had forgotten that you always need at least a day to get your bearings and some proper rest, I can't imagine what I was thinking when I agreed to perform without adequate time to compose myself.

But that didn't matter now. There was little time to get acclimatized so just as well my composer was a wizard. When I first met him in the studio all those years ago, he had impressed me straight away with his musical gifts. In South Africa he had carefully and skillfully laid down the backing tracks to the album using only the best musicians, and it was a similar story here.

While I tried to gather myself, pottering about the room, unpacking, finding my bearings and generally recovering from the flight, my composer was already putting the band through its paces and explaining my requirements to them. Sloppy work wasn't his style, when it came to music he was the ultimate professional. A true perfectionist, only when he was convinced that the players had reached the required musical level and that they had fully understood my musical style did he send for me.

Sound checks are essential to a good performance. There isn't a singer I can think of who would dream of stepping onstage without a proper workout. My road manager in South Africa used to lock away my personal microphone in a briefcase after a rehearsal so that no one else could disturb an atom of our preparation. It wasn't superstition, he regarded it as a precaution: a singer could never be too careful is his explanation for the length he goes to. Now, as the sun bore down in SVG, I was introduced to the backing band. We went through the details of the show, tweaked this and honed that until everyone was satisfied. They were a very professional outfit, I was pleased to see, quick on the uptake and with a beautiful crisp sound. Everything was in place for a smashing event.

It was an evening show, of course, giving us an opportunity to cool off and to prepare for the big event. The timing allowed the public to knock off work, have their meal, shower, then dress for the occasion. From the hotel I could observe the traffic building as the hour approached. The sense of anticipation was fantastic. Hundreds of vehicles, the roads choked, there is no more pleasing sight for a singer or public entertainer. Car after car converging on playing fields where the show was being held, horns blaring, their passengers eager to secure the best position, I could feel the adrenalin rising in my body.

It took me an hour and a half to make what was normally a 10-minute journey. The standing room only venue was packed tight front to back. Thousands had turned out! From the stage all I could see was a sea of red. When the band struck up they went crazy, that's the only way to describe it. 'DD,' they cried, 'DD.' They were like people who had been starved of music and I like to think that we rewarded them for their patience and journey, long or short.

My composer had primed the band and did they respond! We had the audience going for over an hour in the twilight and so were the party faithful. I went home drained but happy, with that serene feeling I get when a show has been particularly well received.

On the ferry to Bequia the Friday I met a member of the opposition. 'Your ears must have been burning, DD,' he said, mischievously. 'We were giving you some real licks.' He said this in jest, it was clear, he wasn't accusing me of selling out or pledging my support for the party. The 'licks' he referred to were obviously verbal, gentle scolding, nothing more. 'I was singing for the people,' I gave the identical reply as I had given when I played before. But it was more complicated than that.

Some years before, I had heard of land for sale in Bequia at a good price. I had written to the former prime minister who was a resident of Bequia. I had met him several times but my letter had gone more in expectation than anything else. To my surprise and delight he had replied, 'Don't worry, leave everything to me.' And, busy though he always is, he had kept his word. He secured me a prime plot, some consider it to be a piece of the best on the island. Now, then, after doing a show for his political rival, as the ferry neared Bequia and with my exchange of words from that member of the opposition, at the back of my mind, I prayed that I wouldn't bump into the prime minister.

Mainland St Vincent is tiny; Bequia is a dot to the south. I hoped by that time news of the show would have died down and some other event would be in the spotlight. No such luck. For there that very day I spotted him on the docks waiting for the ferry. Ah well, I said to myself, you're a musician, you have to face the music sometimes.

'How are you?' the prime minister asked with a twinkle in his eye. 'Hope you're keeping well.' We exchanged greetings, talked a little about this and that then with a grin he said he noticed that I've been campaigning for the other side. I explained that I sang to entertain, that I left politics to the politicians. Then I remember him saying he hoped I got a damn good pay packet too.

On hearing this and noticing his non-judgmental attitude, I wished that ordinary Vincentians could have witnessed our conversation, for we still have a long way to go when it comes to politics. Too many of us put all our faith in one political party and refuse to open our eyes to the achievements of its rivals. We worship the leaders and we despise our neighbours if they don't share our political views. To me this has to change.

The prime minister and I meet regularly at the local supermarket in Bequia, we're on very good terms, you couldn't wish for a better neighbour.

CHAPTER EIGHTEEN

Performing

TO PERFORM FOR AN AUDIENCE, no matter how modest, is a nerve-racking business. No matter how many times you've done it each new show is like putting yourself through hell once more. Nerves, butterflies, the fear of a dud night, there is no worse feeling for a singer than waiting in the wings. You hear the build-up, the hushed expectation of the audience. The roar of anticipation makes its way to the chair, desk, pole or wall you're clasping for quiet support. For an instant you feel light, weightless, the stomach as empty as a tired nomad's.

The first step in the direction of the stage and the butterflies begin to disperse. The surge of adrenalin is like being kicked from the starting line of a 100-metre race to the finishing tape quicker than a dozen Usain Bolts. Within seconds, as the comforting familiarity of the backing track of one of your songs floods the stage, your feet are stepping, your body has absorbed the energy of the tune, and you're ready to fly with the music. You entertain with all your might, rewarding an audience for doling out their hard-earned cash, knowing that the butterflies will reappear at the next show. And the one after that.

Music has been good to me, of that there can be no doubt. There have been hardships along the way but I would be small and ungrateful to dwell on those and ignore the treasure of experiences I have collected over the years, thanks to my contribution to the field of entertainment. My songs still give pleasure to thousands, the number of internet 'hits' on videos of my performances mount steadily. The people I have met on my travels, the mesmerizing countries I have visited, how much of this would have happened if my mother hadn't managed to persuade me to have a go at recording all those years ago?

After the massive hit records and appearances on Top of The Pops, I gave up factory work. That phase of my life was behind me, I swore, the packer and machinist days were over. In between my administrative job and caring for my children, I followed a career of recording, promotion and personal appearances. A singer's life, in other words.

To say that this career has earned me a fortune would be far from the truth. Had it brought me riches I would have given up the council job without having to think of it. Yet, thanks to the popularity of my music, I have managed to keep the wolves from the door. Royalties still trickle in, but live appearances have been my main source of income.

These have taken me across the length and breadth of Great Britain and in Europe, to Holland, Switzerland, France, Belgium and Greece. To think that before I had only been to Europe once, and that was for a day trip! In the Caribbean I have appeared in Jamaica, Grenada and St Lucia. In Central America, Belize and Nicaragua. And I mustn't forget Brazil and the USA.

After 10 albums I think it's fair to say that my music has stood the test of time. To hear that a new generation is growing to appreciate the mellow tunes I laid down over a span of almost 30 years is most gratifying. With so many choices, so many types of media and access to the internet, that youngsters are discovering the songs their parents grew up with can make me choke with emotion. Most of my work has been solo but I have recorded duets too.

Mine has been a full life, I like to think, but hardly the proverbial bed of roses. Money has been a major worry; I suppose I have never completely gotten over the horror of returning from the safe house and being confronted with a mountain of bills. The thought that I was about to lose the precious roof over our heads had brought on feelings I would never like to experience again.

But I don't want to give the impression that money has ever been my motivation. Far from it. There were years when I was in constant demand, yes, busy every fortnight if not each weekend, but equally, there were lean times when performing dried up and I sat morosely at home wondering what the future held. And even when I was busy touring, the kind of sums involved were nowhere like the astronomical figures some people imagine.

To give an example, one of my most lucrative tours was for two shows in the United Arab Emirates. The shows were on consecutive nights and lasted 30 minutes each. Enjoyable they were as well, very much so. The contract shows that I was paid a total of £1500. To me that is quite a tidy amount. When you take into account that my flights, hotel and travel were also provided it would be churlish to say that I didn't get a good deal. That was then, you might say, what about something more up to date? Well, I performed at an entertainment center in Grenada and my fee was US$2000.

But the reality was that I have prospered from record sales, a series of personal appearances and annual visits to South Africa, Uganda, St Lucia and Grenada. These appearances have taken me to all corners of the globe, as the saying goes. I was on the bill of a famous auditorium, where I performed with some of SVG's most illustrious entertainers. One of our ablest comedians entertained the crowd royally that night. Sadly, he died aged 58 in January 2007.

Of all the places I have performed, Nicaragua must be one of the most unusual and memorable. Before my visit there in August 2000, I would have struggled to point it out on a map of the world. It was in Central America: those facts were the only two to spring to mind when the invitation to tour there came. Someone had contacted him about the possibility of a trip and he had relayed the message to me, but I doubt whether he had a better grip on the place than me.

It was a Spanish-speaking country, was my first thought, with perhaps a sprinkling of the languages of the indigenous Indians, similar to one of the South American countries, say, Venezuela. I know that records sometimes take off in far off countries, surprising both the singer and distributor, but I couldn't see how any of mine could have struck a chord (as it were) with people who speak another language thousands of miles away from England. But, my composer said he had been assured, the song had taken off there and, as in South Africa, there was a sizeable population clamouring for me.

I gave the go ahead. Work was work, I wasn't going to let my sketchy knowledge of a country hold me back. I suppose I had developed a love of adventure by then and the prospect of reaching out to thousands of new fans in Central America gave me the kind of thrill singers thrive on. Had the internet been widespread at the time I would have raced to it to do a little research, but back then it was a question of trusting our instincts and hoping that the talk of the popularity of my records hadn't been exaggerated.

We travelled overnight and arrived in the capital, Managua, the third largest city in Central America. We stayed there for four days in a gorgeous hotel, acclimatized, and attended the most lavish parties while we did so. The food was excellent, the music had a wonderfully exotic flavour. Our hosts kept us sweet. 'Now,' they announced at the end of this period of settling in, 'now, we're going to Bluefields.' I had never heard of the place; we had no idea of the distance involved or who the fans were. That, however, is the lot of a singer. You need to have the capacity to turn up at a venue, rehearse, then switch on in unfamiliar surroundings when required.

I regret to say that Bluefields came as a shock. Not in an unpleasant way, but unexpected all the same. After Managua, which is home to people of a multi-ethnic mixture of the descendants of indigenous Indians, Europeans, Africans and Middle Easterners, the shock of an almost entirely black population took several minutes to sink in. What was this place, I asked myself when I could draw breath, was it some concoction of the imagination? A red-carpet welcome had been laid out and a 20-gun salute, but these seemed at odds with the first impressions of the place. The surroundings lacked the glamour of the capital –no surprise there – but the welcome of the people made up for this 100 times over.

To say that I was temporarily fazed would be an understatement. I had assumed that there would be a sprinkling of black people in this distant city, we had been preparing for a similar cosmopolitan mix to the capital. Had the entire black population travelled just to hear us?

I would later discover Nicaragua's connection with the wider English-speaking Caribbean. The original inhabitants of African descent had been added to in the middle of the 20th century by men from the islands who had emigrated to cut sugar cane. These men had settled there, we were told, and, in due course, had sent for their families. Bluefields was the country's main Caribbean port, its population was almost 100,000. No wonder they spoke English the way I did, ate the same food, dressed with the same West Indian panache. Bluefields is home to this Caribbean concentration: the music, dance, storytelling and other traditions resemble ours to a remarkable extent.

So in most respects Bluefields was just like SVG. There was one huge difference though, and we soon felt it. The heat bore down on the land with a vengeance. For days it was so hot our party was uncomfortable and irritable. Our rooms were in the basement of the hotel and, for some reason, the showers served only cold water. Not simply cold, but freezing. Imagine feeling hot and sticky and not being able to cool down and refresh. The coldness of the showers became our in-joke. 'Did you do it?' we asked each other each morning when we met up, 'did you?' And the answer was always the same, 'No', with a childish titter to add spice to the response.

Eventually I gave in, braced myself and let the water do its work. Top and tail could only last this long, I needed to feel the rush of water over my entire body. The night before the show I was out for the count. I developed a cold, I had a sore throat, I was as miserable as can be. A doctor was called, he gave me antibiotics and I bought a throat spray and tried to get myself into some kind of physical shape and in the right frame of mind. So long a wait, and now this. I crossed my fingers, prayed and hoped that the show would go well. All that time preparing mentally, the thousands who would have travelled great distances for the show, and there I was a physical wreck!

And there was a further worry on the day of the show itself. We had noticed it but, as foreigners, hadn't fully worked out the pattern: heat and rain, rain and heat. The heat was tremendous, the rain something to behold. The heavens would open and down tumbled the rain with all its might. Living in England for so long, I assumed that these downpours were somehow extraordinary. The idea that they descended with such ferocity all season didn't seem credible. 'Hope it rains today,' the locals said, shaking their heads knowingly, meaning that they were praying that it rained during daytime. 'Because if it doesn't rain today it will certainly come tonight.' I crossed my fingers and prayed.

The stadium was massive and it was packed. Heaving with people would probably be a better description. Everyone had come dressed in their finest, they were determined to make the show one to remember. It was a fascinating sight. There is nothing more satisfying than a crowd primed for the night, marking the occasion with colour, noise and the determination to have a great time.

A Jamaican singer who had moved to England to further her career was also on the bill. Her easy style is similar to mine, some say, our repertoire consists of love songs, tales of loss and hope and tender longings. She had been looking forward to performing and she was good. Her act flowed easily, she blended her beautiful voice to the music with such little effort that you had to admire her skill.

The 30,000 people who had made the trip were definitely having their money's worth.

As she was nearing the end of her set, the rain began. And, as the locals had predicted this was no simple shower. It was as though the sky had been dammed and had caved in under the pressure. Down thudded the rain with a tremendous roar. I'm not a great fan of rain at the best of times and she finished her set I said to myself, there's no way I'm going out there. And I meant it. Not when I wasn't in the best of health, not when I had just had my hair done, not when I was wearing one of my expensive dresses.

'What are you waiting for?' the sponsor asked as I stood by the stage like a child afraid to dip her toe in the water. By this time the crowd was in frenzy. They were like people impervious to the weather. 'DD,' I could hear them chanting. 'DD'

What was I supposed to do? They had travelled miles, had spent their money, had probably bought new clothes. Every single one had to be soaked through and through. If thousands were prepared to stand there drenched, how could I disappoint them? To hell with the rain, I said, bracing myself, to hell with my dress and hair. So on I went to a thundering reception.

I began. I launched into my routine and soon had them at fever pitch. Rain or no rain music had to come first. They danced. They recognized each song and cheered long and hard, the dancing became hotter and hotter, the evening funkier. The rain didn't ease, but now at least I had some protection for this man appeared with the most enormous umbrella imaginable and held it over me as I sang. Each shift, each sway and he followed me, keeping out the rain as best he could. It had to be one of the weirdest feelings in all my years of performing! An entire set in a rainstorm with the audience dancing and cheering as though it was bright sunshine. And that night at Bluefields the party didn't stop after our acts. The festivities carried on for hours with people seeming to dance in the mud. I was told that the enjoyment would only end when it was daybreak.

In Grenada too, where I have appeared annually, I am told that the audience remains after the show and dance the night away. Music has that impact on people; music and dance are surely two of our greatest pleasures.

CHAPTER NINETEEN

Retirement

I TOOK EARLY RETIREMENT IN 2011. Sixty seemed to me a good age to call it a day. I had been working since I arrived in England at 16 and I had had enough of waking up early to drag myself through the cold mornings to earn a crumb and falling asleep on the settee in front of the television in the evening. The current generation has to plod on till they're nearly 70, I feel sorry for them now that I'm a lady of leisure. No, I went early and I have no regrets. I had built a house in Bequia, a wonderful home capable of accommodating the children, grandchildren and friends. My plan is to spend the winter months in the Caribbean sunshine and part of the year in England. Most of my relatives and friends are still based there so I won't cut my ties completely.

Having spent most of my life in England I was well aware that I was leaving behind the people I had grown up with and the scenes of so many precious memories of youth and adulthood there. And, of course, I would take with me to my new home not just the precious memories, but also the evidence of a successful musical career.

My friends from primary school in Dickson are scattered north, south and west, if not east. I would have to begin afresh in SVG, I knew, but that didn't worry me. Challenges are there to be faced, I told myself, I had dealt with the trials I had come up against, and I would do the same again.

My home in Bequia sits on a hill overlooking the beach. It's a lovely three-bedroom house with a side garage, a design of which I'm truly proud. It is a two-storey building with a cobblestone front with an arched front entrance. The rear of the house faces the sea. Modest by Vincentian standards, it suits me fine. The living room is spacious, allowing a gentle breeze to course through, the kitchen equipped with the most modern appliances.

In the distance, unless there is a rainstorm, I wake up to a gorgeous view of the tiny islands of Balliceau and Battowia, grey and beautiful in the early morning, half-remembered pages of history. The lushness of the vegetation that surrounds the house on three sides, the green boughs of the coconut trees by the sea, the quiet of the landscape, it is a tremendous sight to greet the eye as you ease your way into early morning. A light breeze cools the rooms when the sun strikes fierce, I could sit on one of the outdoor chairs at the back of my home and fall asleep with little persuasion.

Bequia is like a village; in many ways it reminds me of Dickson. Most of the residents know each other; it is a warm community in every sense. People are polite; they look out for one another. With its own airport and a tiny but functional capital, the island is a typical Caribbean retreat. Most of the conveniences of Europe are at our disposal, Bequia is modern and a great tourist attraction. It's a favourite holiday destination for people from the mainland. At Easter, Christmas and bank holidays the ferry is packed, everyone comes for the beaches and the swimming cannot be faulted.

I have always fancied myself as a gardener and now I can invest more time in cultivating my little garden. With my headscarf or little cap keeping out the sun, I plant tomatoes, cabbages and spring onions. I can't think of anything more relaxing. Flowers are next, crotons, dragon's blood, some ferns, I imagine; plants that take to the hard, dry earth of a tiny islet. Then it will be time to graduate to a plum tree, or mango, and in time I hope to have my own little coconut trees in the yard.

But these will be difficult for Bequia is dry. There are no rivers to splash in, water has to be treated like the precious commodity it is in many parts of the world. Unlike other islands we have our fair share of rain so I mustn't grumble. Despite the hard earth I wouldn't swap my life here for another spot in the world. It is peaceful, tranquil, just the kind of place to reflect and be at peace with myself.

People recognize me and want to know my story; those who don't are respectful and polite towards a stranger. I miss my children and grandchildren but, with the internet and modern communication, we keep in close contact. Friends occasionally drop by, taking the ferry from mainland St Vincent, and I'm happy to accommodate anyone who wants to talk about music, life in England, or any topic (except politics) over a glass of wine.

And, with a little persuasion I would show them round the home I've built on my dream island. They would see my records and achievements decorated about the house not out of vanity, but to remind me of the life I had, bad times as well as good. If they have the time, I would suggest to them that adversities are there to be overcome, and I believe I'm suitably qualified to dispense this gentle prescription. I've been fortunate, I would say, far more fortunate than most people. For who has been privileged as I have to meet singers, performers, entertainers, ministers and royalty in the course of their work?

Music has given me the opportunity to travel to countries most people can only dream of. It has opened doors to places that remain locked to the public. I've met my singing heroes and heroines, the honours I have received still make my heart swell. Platinum and gold discs decorate my walls as do the honorary citizenships I have been granted.

In November 2003 a proclamation by a city council honoured me for my contribution to music. I had distinguished myself as one of reggae's most versatile and successful singers, I was a devoted mother and consummate professional, it read. The proclamation ends by saying that I was an inspiration for all women from the Caribbean. It's difficult for me to read those words without tears welling up.

Sandwiched between the gold and platinum discs is a selection of the other honours for my work. I received a Performance and Music Award in recognition of my commitment, positive and knowledgeable approach and exceptional service in meeting the needs of the people and communities of Brooklyn, New York. I was honoured and recognized in 2011 during the Caribsplash Group Easter Nostalgia. But perhaps the most prestigious of these awards is the one I received in October of the same year.

The occasion was the anniversary of the independence. In a ceremony which was attended by many dignitaries, I was awarded the Certificate of Honour. The award was for my contribution to the development of SVG and for my services to the Vincentian diaspora in the United Kingdom. How could I not be moved by such an honour? How could someone from a tiny village in a tiny country not give thanks for the life she had been given?

But, despite the awards and the recognition I have been accorded, the family photos are the dearest to me. When I sit at home relaxing with a small glass of wine, I say to myself, 'DD girl, you haven't done too bad. Not bad at all.' And I would get up and look lovingly at the photographs of my family, and especially those of my children and grandchildren. The graduation pictures are my favourites, which parent isn't proud of their children's accomplishments? When I recall the experiences, we had and the way my children have managed to triumph over them, I feel proud to be a mother of my daughter, an accomplished chartered accountant and a mother of two; and my son a linguist and father of one.

www.ingramcontent.com/pod-product-compliance
Lightning Source LLC
LaVergne TN
LVHW021712060526
838200LV00050B/2630